**A Critiquing Approach
to Expert Computer
Advice: ATTENDING**

Perry L Miller
Department of Anesthesiology, Yale University

A Critiquing Approach to Expert Computer Advice: ATTENDING

Pitman Advanced Publishing Program

BOSTON · LONDON · MELBOURNE

PITMAN PUBLISHING LIMITED
128 Long Acre, London WC2E 9AN

PITMAN PUBLISHING INC
1020 Plain Street, Marshfield, Massachusetts 02050

Associated Companies
Pitman Publishing Pty Ltd, Melbourne
Pitman Publishing New Zealand Ltd, Wellington
Copp Clark Pitman, Toronto

© Perry L Miller 1984

First published 1984

Library of Congress Cataloging in Publication Data

Miller, Perry L.
  A critiquing approach to expert computer advice—
ATTENDING.

  "Pitman advanced publishing program."
  Bibliography: p.
  Includes index.
  1. Medicine—Decision making—Data processing.
2. Medical logic.   3. Anesthesiology—Decision making—
Data processing.   I. Title.
R858.M54   1984   610'.28'54   84-19017
ISBN 0-273-08665-0

British Library Cataloguing in Publication Data

Miller, Perry L.
  A critiquing approach to expert computer
  advice: ATTENDING.—(Research notes in
  artificial intelligence)
  1. Anesthesia—Data processing
  I. Title   II. Series
  617'.96'02854   RD80.95

  ISBN 0-273-08665-0

Reproduced and printed by photolithography
in Great Britain by Biddles Ltd, Guildford

Contents

9. Current Status and Future Directions

1 Introduction

This book discusses a different approach to computer-based advice: a
critiquing approach. It is anticipated that the critiquing approach may
prove to be particularly well suited for domains which involve a great deal
of subjective judgement.

In particular, the book describes ATTENDING, a computer system designed
using Artificial Intelligence (AI) techniques to critique a physician's
plan for a patient's anesthetic management. In anesthesiology, as in most
of medicine, the decisions a physician makes involve a substantial amount
of subjective judgement at several levels.

1.1 THE CRITIQUING APPROACH

The traditional approach to computer-assisted medical decision-making has
been to design a system which simulates a medical expert's decision making
process. Indeed, this had been the usual approach to building expert
systems in any domain.

Such a system gathers data as an expert would, and then attempts to come
to similarly expert conclusions. When applied to medical management, this
traditional approach has the clinical effect of trying to tell a physician
what to do, how to practice medicine.

In contrast, a critiquing system like ATTENDING assumes that the
physician has already evaluated a patient, and has already formulated
certain thoughts as to management. Rather than attempt to duplicate this
decision-making process, ATTENDING critiques it, discussing the pros and
cons of the proposed approach as compared to alternatives which might be
reasonable or preferred. As a result, whereas the more traditional system
says in effect, "This is how I think you should manage your patient.", the
critiquing system says, "This is what I think of your management plan."

In this way, instead of arbitrarily advocating one approach to a
patient's management, ATTENDING lets the physician be its guide, and
tailors its advice to his thinking and his proposed plan. Indeed, this is
how a physician usually asks another physician for advice. He evaluates

his patient, assesses the available data as fully as possible, and only then does he ask a colleague or a consultant for advice.

The critiquing approach has implications both for computer science and for medicine as a modality for computer advice:

Computer science The critiquing approach is relevant to the field of expert system design. Critiquing represents a different mode for using an expert system's knowledge base. Indeed, as discussed later, critiquing can be seen as a form of explanation, with the advantage that it focuses the system's analysis around the particular concerns of the user in a very direct and natural way.

Medicine The critiquing approach also has potential social, medical, and medicolegal advantages as a modality for advice. It may have similar advantages in any field in which decisions involve a significant degree of subjective judgement.

The remainder of this chapter discusses the clinical rationale for critiquing in more detail.

1.2 CLINICAL ADVANTAGES OF THE CRITIQUING APPROACH

The primary motivation for exploring the critiquing approach is a conviction that it brings advice to the physician in the form which he can most productively use. There are several potential clinical advantages to critiquing a physician's proposed plan rather than trying to tell him what to do, including:

Acceptability The approach casts the computer in the role of the physician's ally, rather than as a potential competitor. To the extent that a physician feels threatened by computer technology, this role may prove more acceptable.

The physician must think the problem through himself The approach also forces the physician to grapple with the problem himself, and think through any difficult management issues, before turning to the computer for assistance. Thus it keeps the physician centrally involved in the decision-making process.

Medicine is very subjective   A physician develops his own idiosyncratic style of practice, and would have little use for a computer-advisor which did not let him practice medicine in his accustomed fashion.   There are frequently several ways to approach a particular problem, and it is seldom that one approach is "right", and the others are "wrong".   Indeed, even an approach that is in some sense "suboptimal" may be best for a physician most familiar with that way of doing things.

Nuances in a given patient   Also, there are frequently nuances in a given patient which are hard to anticipate and difficult to quantify, but which lead a physician to lean one way or another in a patient's management. Here again, evaluation of these factors can be a very subjective process. Physicians frequently assess such "nuances" differently, and are therefore led to take different management approaches to the same patient.

Medicolegal issues   Finally, granting the practical forces which operate in contemporary medicine, it makes both medical and medicolegal sense to leave the major responsibility and decision-making with the physician and let the computer play a secondary role.   The computer can help the physician evaluate and optimize _his_ approach.

Thus there are a number of practical reasons why the critiquing approach may be particularly well suited to medicine.   In particular, critiquing may help avoid certain potential social, medical, and medicolegal problems which may confront a computer system which tries to dictate how a physician should practice medicine.

1.3   THE SEEDS OF CRITIQUING: SOURCES OF SUBJECTIVITY

Beyond these reasons for advocating the critiquing approach in _medicine_, the approach may also prove useful in any domain in which decisions involve subjective judgement.   Subjective elements enter into most of the decisions of daily life.   This subjectivity has many sources.

Sources of subjectivity in medicine include:

The institution(s) where a physician has trained   Different institutions
frequently have their own school of thought as to how particular problems
are best handled.   In the course of his training (which could include
medical school, internship, residency, and fellowship), a physician may
train at several different institutions, and may therefore emerge with his
own unique blend of the various philosophies to which he has been exposed.

Standards of care in a community   Different communities have different
standards of care, as well as different resources available for delivery of
care.   The practice of medicine in a major teaching hospital may be very
different from that in a small, remote community.   For that matter,
different hospitals and clinics have different drugs available in their
formularies, and different tests available in their laboratories.

A physician's personal practice experiences   Perhaps the ultimate
determinant of a physician's personal practive preferences, of course, is
his individual experience of what has and has not worked well for him in
the past.

Medical knowledge is constantly in flux   Finally, underlying all these
other factors, is the fluid, changing nature of clinical science.   New
drugs, tests, and procedures are constantly being developed and refined.
These diffuse at different rates into practice.   Also, studies are
constantly being published evaluating the relative efficacy of different
techniques.   This constant evolution of medical knowledge means that the
practice of medicine is constantly changing.   An important role a computer
can play is to help bring this evolving knowledge to the physician in an
organized way, focused around his present style of practice.

As a result of these factors, there is tremendous practice variation
among physicians.   This in turn makes the practice of medicine a very
personal, subjective process.   Clearly, this situation is not unique to
medicine.   There are many areas of life where decision-making is subject to
similar variation and subjectivity.

4

In a subjective domain, there are three fundamental ways one might structure computer advice:

Advocating a "best" approach   The computer might try to dictate the best approach to take. As outlined above, this approach has major drawbacks in a subjective domain.

A general discussion   The computer might produce a general discussion of the issues involved. This general discussion could outline reasonable approaches which might be taken, and discuss the relative risks and benefits of each. There are, however, disadvantages to such a general analysis. First, a general discussion runs the risk that it might lack a focus. Also, if the user were contemplating a poorly conceived approach, the general discussion might not adequately address his errors.

Critiquing   The third alternative is the critiquing approach. Here, the user's plan provides a natural focus for the discussion. This in turn allows the computer's analysis to be structured directly to the user's frame of reference.

From the standpoint of the user, there is a great deal of logic to the type of focussed feedback that critiquing provides. A general discussion of alternatives is not likely to have the same impact as focused feedback structured directly around one's own thinking.

1.4 CRITIQUING: ADVICE IN AN AREA OF PREEXISTING USER COMPETENCE

Implicit in the critiquing approach is the assumption that the user is fundamentally competent in the field being critiqued. He must be able to generate a plan of his own and evaluate the system's critique appropriately. At first glance, this assumption of preexisting user competence may seem to limit the approach. One might, for instance, want to develop an expert system to assist the physician in areas where he felt uncertain or inadequate. Unfortunately, this approach ignores medical reality.

In medicine, a specialty consultant is much more than a source of information for a primary physician. A consultant is someone to whom a physician can pass responsibility when confronted by a problem where he feels beyond his depth. In private practice, the consultant frequently takes over that aspect of the patient's care.

Frequently a primary physician calls in a consultant when he does not want to deal with a problem, and wants to pass medical and legal responsibility for that problem to someone else. If instead of using a human consultant, the primary physician utilizes a computer in an area of relative ignorance, he is forced to manage the patient's problem himself. He must therefore take the medical and legal responsibility upon himself as well. He must sign the orders.

A successful computer-advisor is therefore probably best designed to give assistance in a domain where the physician has the basic competence to evaluate the advice given, and is ready to take full responsibility for the patient's care. A computer cardiology advisor, for example, would therefore be designed to assist a cardiologist, or to assist the primary physician only in some aspect of cardiac management where he was expected to be fundamentally competent.

For these reasons, therefore, the assumption of preexisting user competence is probably not a major restriction on the critiquing approach in medicine. Instead it reflects the reality of the role which the computer can be expected to play.

1.5 AN OVERVIEW FOR THE READER

One of the exciting features of an interdisciplinary field like medical computing is the diversity of background which people bring to the field. This diversity does, however, pose a problem when presenting material, since the potential audience may include people with great knowledge in either field and virtually none in the other.

People interested in reading about a system like ATTENDING might have backgrounds in artificial intelligence, computer science, medical computing, medicine, and anesthesiology. Some may know little about computers. Others may know little about medicine. Only a very specific subgroup will know anything about anesthesiology.

As a result of this diversity, an attempt has been made to keep the presentation as clear and readable as possible, and to include short introductory sections wherever it seemed appropriate.

Chapter 1 outlines the critiquing approach which ATTENDING implements, and puts the approach in perspective from a medical standpoint.

Chapter 2 discusses the fields of AI in general and of expert systems in particular. The goal of this chapter is to help put critiquing into perspective from the standpoint of these two fields, and especially with regard to other research on the application of AI in medicine.

Chapter 3 introduces the field of anesthesiology. It also describes the ATTENDING system in overview, giving examples of the system's operation and an outline of the system design.

Chapters 4-6 describe the details of ATTENDING's current implementation. In particular, these three chapters focus on three central phases of the system's operation: 1) the exploration of alternative approaches to anesthetic management, 2) the evaluation and analysis of the various risks that these alternative approaches might involve, and 3) the generation of ATTENDING's English prose critique of the physcian's plan.

Chapter 7 discusses several of the system's current limitations, and certain interesting features of the critiquing approach as implemented in ATTENDING.

Chapter 8 describes how ATTENDING is currently being used experimentally for teaching using hypothetical cases, while still under development for eventual consultation use with real cases. In addition to its potential educational value, this tutorial use of the system also demonstrates a practical mode for validation and evaluation of an expert knowledge base during its formative stages.

Chapter 9 summarizes the progress of the ATTENDING project to date. It also discusses a number of possible extensions of the critiquing approach, including some projects which are already in progress. Finally, the chapter discusses ways in which the system itself might be further extended and made more sophisticated.

Appendix I shows a teaching session which illustrates how ATTENDING has been adapted for tutorial use. This session also contains additional examples of ATTENDING in operation.

Appendices II and III show some of ATTENDING's internal LISP data structures, illustrating how the system stores its knowledge of anesthetic management alternatives and of medical risks.

2 Background

2.1 ARTIFICIAL INTELLIGENCE

The field of Artificial Intelligence (AI) has grown over the past twenty five years, evolving initially as a subfield of computer science. During this period, AI has received considerable coverage in the popular press, and in the past few years has also attracted substantial interest for commercial applications. This section gives an introductory overview of the field (Winston 1977; Rich 1983).

A precise definition of AI is not easily formulated. AI might be described as the science of making a computer system behave or respond in a manner that appears to exhibit "intelligence". Implicit in this definition is the understanding that a program that performs a purely numerical computation, such as a statistical program, is not AI. Indeed two terms are often used to characterize the nature of AI computation: symbolic and heuristic.

<u>Symbolic computation</u> Rather then manipulating numeric data, AI programs usually manipulate symbols: non-numeric data and data structures that represent non-numeric objects. These symbols may represent concrete objects in the real world such as the components of an automobile or a set of blocks on a table, or more abstract objects such as concepts, states, goals, etc.

<u>Heuristic computation</u> A heuristic solution to a problem is one that cannot be readily reduced to an equation or a well-defined algorithm. Heuristic solutions are therefore sometimes called "weak solutions". Much real-world reasoning seems to require heuristic methods. Indeed AI might be called the science of heuristic problem solving.

The field of AI includes a broad spectrum of different research areas. These include:

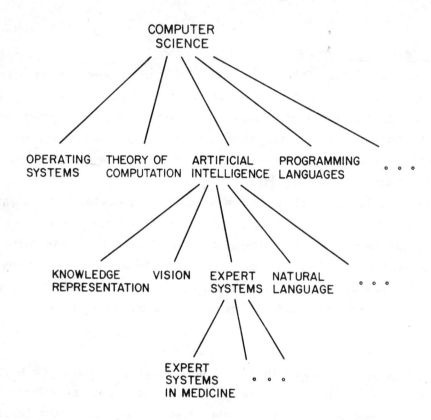

Figure 2.1 Computer science, artificial intelligence, and expert systems.

<u>Game playing</u>   A number of programs have been developed to play sophisticated games such as chess. In fact, a computer recently defeated the world backgammon champion.

<u>Robotics</u>   In its most sophisticated form, a robotics system can sense its surroundings (e.g. using television input), move, and manipulate objects in its environment.

<u>Vision</u>   Vision systems typically take as input the very noisy, two-dimensional image obtained from a television camera, and use a variety of different knowledge about lines, shapes, and objects to deduce the three-dimensional scene being portrayed.

<u>Natural language</u>   A number of projects have worked on the very difficult linguistic problems involved in understanding a "natural" language such as English. Other projects have worked on the similarly challenging task of producing natural language output from a deep semantic representation of concepts to be described.

<u>Expert systems</u>   As discussed more fully in Section 2.2, a rapidly growing field is the development of "expert systems" which embody the expertise of a real world domain.

Underlying the work in these and other areas is more fundamental work on basic AI issues, such as 1) knowledge representation, 2) models of reasoning and of problem solving, 3) heuristic search, 4) learning, 5) the modelling of temporal and spatial relationships, and 6) the development of AI-oriented programming languages.

Work in AI spans a wide range of intellectual disciplines, overlapping such diverse fields as psychology, linguistics, philosophy, mathmatics, and cognitive sciences, in addition to the many fields which have served as domains for the application of AI techniques. The common underlying theme in all this work is an emphasis on symbolic computation, and the development of heuristic solutions to complex problems.

2.1.1 LISP

A discussion of AI is incomplete without at least mentioning LISP (Winston and Horn 1981), the programming language widely used to implement AI systems, including ATTENDING. For a number of reasons, LISP is a very well-designed language for symbolic computation, for the flexible representation of complex data objects, and for the efficient implementation and debugging of large, complex heuristic programs.

2.2 EXPERT SYSTEMS

The field of expert systems is a subfield of AI which has emerged over the past 10-15 years. An expert system is a computer system designed using AI techniques to operate in a real-world domain. Many different domains have been explored, including geologic analysis (Campbell et al. 1982), computer system design (McDermott 1982), and medicine.

The implementation of an expert system typically requires that a human expert in the field interact with a group of computer specialists over a period of time. During this interaction, he works to make his knowledge of the field (his "expertise") explicit, so that it can be incorporated into the computer. This is typically a difficult process, and a substantial amount of reformulation and iteration is usually necessary. The goal is to develop a system which can make expert level judgements and recommendations in the field.

The amount of knowledge required to reach this level of performance can be very large in many real-world domains. As a result, the task of validating the knowledge base, assuring its accuracy and completeness, can itself be a major undertaking.

It is interesting that a great deal of the initial work on expert systems was done in medicine. In fact, in the mid-1970's, the majority of expert systems being developed were medical. In recent years, however, the technology developed in building these systems has spread rapidly to many other areas. As a result, medical systems today comprise only a modest fraction of the expert systems currently implemented.

2.3 EXPERT CONSULTATION SYSTEMS IN MEDICINE

Over the past fifteen years expert consultation systems have been developed in many quite different areas of medicine. (Shortliffe et al. 1979;

12

Kulikowski 1980; Szolovits 1982; Clancey and Shortliffe 1984) Some are diagnostic. Others deal with areas of medical management, as does ATTENDING. Section 2.5 discusses some of the differences between diagnosis and management as domains for computer advice. The systems also differ in the types of capabilities which they attempt to acheive. Section 2.4 discusses some of these capabilities in more detail.

This section gives an overview of a number of well-known medical expert systems.

2.3.1 DENDRAL

DENDRAL (Buchanan and Feigenbaum 1978; Lindsay et al. 1980) is a non-clinical expert system which served as a precursor to certain later lines of expert system research. DENDRAL was developed at Stanford to analyze mass spectrographic and nuclear magnetic resonance data to help in identifying chemical compounds. Since it is able to hypothesize all plausible interpretations of the data, DENDRAL finds structures in a systematic, comprehensive way which humans cannot easily equal.

2.3.2 The MYCIN systems

Certain of the approaches developed in the DENDRAL project were further refined in MYCIN (Shortliffe 1976; Buchanan and Shortliffe 1983), a consultation system developed in the domain of infectious disease. MYCIN explored the use of "production rules" as a medium for knowledge representation, as discussed more fully in Section 2.4. The domain-independent core of MYCIN was then packaged into EMYCIN ("empty" MYCIN) a system for building expert systems. (van Melle 1979) One system built using EMYCIN was PUFF (Aikins et al. 1983), currently in use for interpreting pulmonary function tests.

Two additional projects used the MYCIN infectious disease knowledge base to investigate fundamental aspects of expert system design. The GUIDON/NEOMYCIN project (Clancey and Letsinger 1981; London and Clancey 1982) developed an "expert teaching system" which used MYCIN's knowledge base to explore epistemological issues of sophisticated computer-aided teaching. TEIRESIAS (Davis and Lenat 1982) used MYCIN's rule-based knowledge as a domain to explore issues of knowledge acquisition. This research involved giving a system "meta-knowledge" about its own knowledge,

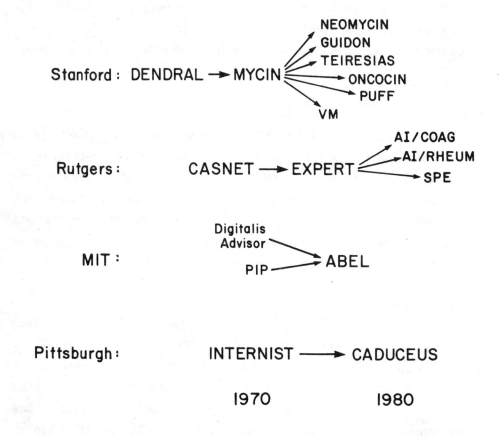

Figure 2.2 An outline of several selected projects developing expert systems in medicine.

so it could actively help a domain expert update its knowledge base. Knowledge acquisition is discussed in Section 2.4

2.3.3 CASNET and EXPERT

Another center of expert system development is at Rutgers. This work started with CASNET (Kulikowski and Weiss 1971), a system which performed diagnosis in ophthalmology. Next EXPERT (Weiss et al. 1978; Weiss and Kulikowski 1979) was developed, a rule-based system designed to facilitate the development of expert systems in different domains. By incorporating appropriate rules, EXPERT has been applied in diverse areas including endocrinology, and in two systems developed collaboratively at the University of Missouri, AI/COAG (Kingsland et al. 1982) whose domain is coagulation/hematology, and AI/RHEUM (Lindberg et al. 1980; Kingsland and Lindberg 1983) which deals with rheumatology.

A recent interesting extension of EXPERT is a "compiler" which allows the system's rules to be translated onto a microchip. (Weiss et al. 1981) Using this process, SPE, a modest-sized rule-based system which interpets serum protein electrophoresis data, has been incorporated into the hardware of a commercial laboratory instrument.

2.3.4 INTERNIST/CADUCEUS

By far the most ambitious project is the INTERNIST/CADUCEUS system (R Miller et al. 1982) under development at the University of Pittsburg, which attempts to embrace the whole of internal medicine. Experimental evaluation of the first developmental prototype (INTERNIST-1) using clinicopathological cases from the New England Journal of Medicine demonstrated impressive preformance. The evaluation, however, also demonstrated the need to incorporate deeper types of knowledge (anatomy, physiology, etc.) into the diagnostic reasoning process. The project is now at work exploring these issues. (Pople 1982)

2.3.5 PIP and the Digitalis Advisor

Another varied set of systems has been developed at MIT in conjunction with Tufts Medical School, and other nearby medical centers. PIP (Pauker et al. 1976) explored diagnostic issues in the domain of renal disease. The Digitalis Advisor (Gorry et al. 1978) focused on medical management in the domain of digitalis therapy. ABEL (Patil et al. 1981) has explored acid base and electrolyte disorders, attempting to develop appropriate deep models of underlying processes to guide the system's analysis.

2.3.6 Several management systems

Most of the work outlined above has focused primarily on medical diagnosis. Some systems, however, have dealt with medical managment, as does ATTENDING. As discussed in Section 2.5, management may prove to be particularly fertile for computer assistance. In addition to the Digitalis Advisor mentioned above, two systems which have focused on management are VM (Fagan et al. 1979) which deals with the ventilatory management of a patient receiving respiratory support, and ONCOCIN (Shortliffe et al. 1981) which helps implement oncology protocols. Both of these systems extend the rule-based approach developed in diagnostic systems into medical management.

Most of the systems outlined above are still in the research and development stages. A very promising development in the past few years, however, is the movement of certain systems into routine use. Two of these, PUFF and SPE, are systems which interpret laboratory test results. They are therefore not true consultation systems since they do not interact with the physician, but rather take instrument readings directly as their input. One system which does interact sucessfully with a physician user is ONCOCIN. In fact, as discussed in Section 2.5, systems like ONCOCIN which assist medical management may be more readily brought to practical use than diagnostic systems. As a result, the first wave of working expert consultation systems may well come in areas of medical management.

ONCOCIN's domain is almost unique in medicine in that oncology "protocols" dictate in detail how oncologic drugs are to be administered. Thus the process of implementing such a protocol is largely objective. The protocol removes most of the practice variation and subjectivity present in other areas of medicine. This indeed may explain in part why ONCOCIN has been sucessful.

It is our hope that the critiquing approach may assist in the development of management advisors in the broader, more subjective areas of medicine where protocols are not used.

2.4 EXPERT SYSTEMS: DESIRED CAPABILITIES

As outlined in Chapter 1, a critiquing capability may prove valuable for an expert system, particularly in a subjective domain. To help put ATTENDING and its critiquing approach into perspective, this section discusses three other capabilities which researchers have worked to incorporate into expert systems: 1) flexibility of knowledge representation, 2) explanation capabilities, and 3) knowledge acquisition capabilities.

2.4.1 Flexibility of knowledge representation

Perhaps the most important desired capability is that an expert system have a very flexible, manipulable knowledge representation. As discussed above, many expert systems acheive this flexibility by storing their knowledge in the standardized form of "production rules".

For instance, the following example rule, taken from the MYCIN system (Shortliffe 1976, p71) illustrates the flexibility that rules allow:

```
PREMISE: ($AND (SAME CNTXT GRAM GRAMPOS)
               (SAME CNTXT MORPH COCCUS)
               (SAME CNTXT CONFORM CLUMPS))
ACTION: (CONCLUDE CNTXT IDENT STAPHYLOCOCCUS TALLY .7)
```

An English translation of the rule is shown below:

```
IF:       1) THE STAIN OF THE ORGANISM IS GRAMPOS, AND
          2) THE MORPHOLOGY OF THE ORGANISM IS COCCUS, AND
          3) THE GROWTH CONFORMATION OF THE ORGANISM IS CLUMPS
THEN:     THERE IS SUGGESTIVE EVIDENCE (.7) THAT THE IDENTITY
          OF THE ORGANISM IS STAPHYLOCOCCUS
```

This rule can be used to make "inferences". If the three conditions in the premise are found to hold, the inference implied by the action can be made. Other rules may include the inference made by this rule as part of their premise. In this way, a chain of inferences can be built up by successive rules, until the system's final conclusions are reached.

A rule-based system contains many such rules. Each rule can be thought of as a "chunk" of knowledge. There are several advantages to structuring knowledge in this form, as compared to a conventional program where knowledge is "procedurally embedded" in sequences of computer instructions.

Ease of understanding   As can be seen in the example, the English translation of the rule is relatively easy to infer from the rule's internal form.   As a result, a medical collaborator can hope to inspect the system's knowledge himself and help debug it, even if he knows little about computer programming.   Were the knowledge "procedurally embedded" in a conventional programming language, it would be much less accessible.

Accessibility to the system itself   With its knowledge stored in this standardized flexible form, not only is it more accessible to the designers, it is also possible for the system to inspect and manipulate the knowledge itself.   In this way, as discussed below, not only can the rules be used to make inferences, they may also greatly facilitate explanation and knowledge acquisition.   Thus, flexibility of knowledge representation is central to expert system design.

Although many expert systems are rule-based, other representations have also been used.   For instance, as discussed earlier, some systems use deep models or causal models to represent their knowledge.   Also, as discussed in Chapter 4, ATTENDING uses the representation of an Augmented Transition Network as the basis of its critiquing analysis.   The main requirement of these different forms of knowledge representation is that they be flexible, and well suited for the type of capabilities their designers hope to acheive.

2.4.2 Explanation
A second desired capability is that an expert system be able to explain its internal logical processes to the user.   (Swartout 1981; Scott et al. 1983). In particular, it should be able to explain:

(a) why it is pursuing a certain line of questioning, and
(b) why it has made a certain recommendation.

In fact, a recent study (Teach and Shortliffe 1981) investigated physician attitudes toward medical consultation systems. The conclusions of this study were interesting in that the physicians queried did not insist that the computer always be right. They apparently felt that this was too much to ask of any expert, human or otherwise. They did feel, however, that it was critical that the computer be able to explain its recommendations so that the physician could evaluate the advice he was given.

There are a number of possible ways to approach the design of such an explanation capability. In a rule-based system, the rules can be used directly for this purpose.

(a) In a rule-based system, the rules are frequently used to direct the questioning of the user. As a result, were the physician to query why a certain question was asked, the system could reply with the English translation of the rule involved. ("I am asking this question because if (premise of the rule), then (action of the rule).")

(b) Similarly, if the physician queried one of the system's inferences, the system could justify it by quoting the English translation of the rule which yielded that inference. Indeed, if necessary, the physician could start with the system's final conclusions and ask successively "why...why...why..." and in this way trace back through the entire chain of inferences which had been made.

As can be seen, this form of explanation allows a physician to ask <u>why</u> the system has made a conclusion. It may, however, be limited in its ability to let him ask <u>why not</u> take a different approach, although certain types of "why not" questions can be dealt with (Davis and Lenat 1982). Questions as to "why not" may be very important to the physician. The critiquing approach may prove helpful in this regard.

2.4.2.1 <u>Critiquing as a mode of explanation</u>
As outlined above, an explanation capability allows a user to inquire why the system is pursuing a certain line of questioning, and why certain conclusions and recommendations are made. The goal is to help make the

computer's logical processes transparent, so that the user can evaluate the advice he is given. An explanation capability therefore allows the system's advice to be adapted to the particular questions and concerns of the physician, using the computer's recommendations as a starting point.

A much more direct way to adapt the computer's analysis to the user's thinking, however, is to use a different approach to advice-giving: the critiquing approach. Here, instead of initially telling the physician what to do, the system first asks what approach he is contemplating, and then critiques that plan. This mode of advice immediately focuses the system's analysis around the particular concerns of the physician in a very natural and direct way. Thus critiquing can be seen as a particular form of explanation.

2.4.3 Knowledge acquisition

A third desired capability is that an expert system be able to assist in the modification of its own knowledge. (Davis and Lenat 1982) In the long run, this may prove to be a critical capability. Real-world expertise has a number of very interesting characteristics which make such "knowledge acquisition" important.

Completeness may only be approached asymptotically No human expert or group of experts can ever know everything about their domain of expertise. As a result, no expert system can be expected to know everything either, especially since there are practical limits on the extraction of knowledge from a human expert. At some point, the law of diminishing returns sets in. As a result, one may periodically come upon additional knowledge which must be added to the system. Completeness of an expert system's knowledge base can probably only be approached asymptotically.

Medical knowledge evolves This practical barrier to making an expert system's knowledge complete is heightened by the fact that medical knowledge is not static. Rather, it constantly evolves. New drugs, tests, and procedures frequently become available. New studies are performed evaluating the relative efficacy of different approaches to a problem. An expert system must therefore be updated as the field itself evolves.

As a result of this evolution of real-world expertise, an expert system differs greatly from a more conventional program. The expert system's knowledge must constantly change to reflect the evolution of human knowledge. The ultimate solution to this problem is to have the computer help update itself. Work on knowledge acquisition is currently still largely developmental. It is clear, however, that a flexible knowledge representation, such as production rules, can greatly facilitate the process.

2.4.4 Summary

In summary, the designers of expert systems have a number of ambitious capabilities which they would like their systems to acheive. Critiquing is such a capability, and can be seen as a form of explanation. It can be thought of as a control strategy which allows a different type of interaction between a user and an expert knowledge base.

2.5 MANAGEMENT VS. DIAGNOSIS AS AN AREA FOR COMPUTER ADVICE

As outlined in section 2.3, much of the previous work applying AI in medicine has focused on diagnosis. This may be because diagnosis is perceived by the layman as the salient intellectual activity in medicine. Diagnosis has provided a test ground for a large number of very interesting systems.

In contrast, ATTENDING focuses on problems of medical management, as have several other AI systems. To help put this aspect of the system into perspective, this section presents several arguments as to why medical management may prove a more tractable domain for the development of practical computer advisors than diagnosis. These arguments may be controversial. They are presented to help enhance the reader's appreciation of the goals of the ATTENDING project.

In particular, this section discusses some of the difficulties of diagnosis as a domain for medical consultation systems, and some of the advantages of medical management.

2.5.1 The problems with diagnosis

Diagnosis poses a number of problems as a practical domain for computer advice:

Many problems are chronic A large proportion of the patients a doctor sees
have chronic medical problems which fluctuate in severity. When one of
these patients comes to a physician, the presumptive diagnosis is already
known.

Subtle clues may point to underlying problems Many missed diagnoses occur
because a physician does not pursue fully enough the underlying cause of
known problems. The clues suggesting that deeper investigation might be
appropriate in a given patient may be subtle and quite subjective, and
therefore difficult to specify objectively.

Certainly when a patient has a number of clear-cut findings which a
physician cannot integrate with one another, a computer could be of great
help by matching these findings against a broad range of rare syndromes and
uncommon presentations of common disease. Such patients, however, are
relatively rare. As a result, a diagnostic system could be expected, at
best, to help with a small fraction of the patients a physician sees.

Diagnostic systems have the further problem that they may often require
a wide range of information. To do diagnosis thoroughly, even in a
restricted domain, a broad spectrum of possible questions may be relevant.
Some of the current diagnostic systems require 30 minutes or more to gather
this data. It is probably unrealistic to expect a physician to tolerate
such a large demand on his time.

2.5.2 The advantages of medical management
Medical management (taken here to mean treatment in its broadest sense)
does not have many of these problems. Many chronic patients whose
diagnosis is well established may still present very difficult and
challenging management problems. Also, by concentrating on the management
of well-defined problems, the interaction with the physician can often be
much more focused, and therefore less time-consuming. For instance,
interaction with the ATTENDING system takes a minute or so.

Another feature of medical management that makes computer assistance
especially useful is the intermittent concentration it demands of the
physician. Whereas the bulk of diagnostic reasoning takes place when a
patient is first encountered, management is a longer term, incremental

process. For a given patient, management decisions typically occur once or twice a day as the physician makes rounds in the hospital, or weekly to monthly on an outpatient basis.

Granting this intermittent nature of management, the computer offers the advantage that it can easily remember all the relevant considerations from one encounter to another. It can therefore play a useful role if only by making sure the physician has not forgotten, overlooked, or failed to think through the full implications of a particular patient's individual set of problems.

2.5.3 A pharmacy system as an example

An example of a management system may help illustrate these advantages. A well-established application is a pharmacy system which checks a patient's medication orders against allergies, against such things as renal failure, and for possible drug-drug interactions. Even though such a system does not typically use AI techniques, it does illustrate clearly the advantages of management as a domain for computer advice.

(a) The scope of the system's interaction is narrow and limited: it need only know a patient's medications, plus a small amount of other information such as allergies, major organ disease, and perhaps sex, age, and weight. Most of this information need only be entered initially. As a result, an interaction with the system can be very focused and brief.

(b) During an extended course of treatment, a physician may change a patient's medications many times. In so doing, he may not always consider the patient as a whole: for example, all the potential drug-drug interactions that may occur. The methodical computer can keep these factors in mind and can therefore be of significant assistance in preventing inadvertent errors.

With the help of AI techniques, this basic process of cross-checking a physician's proposed plan of treatment can be extended to other, more complex areas of medical management as well.

2.5.4 Advantages of anesthetic management

Anesthesiology is an excellent domain for exploring these issues of computer-assisted management for several reasons:

(a) Anesthesia has a central management component.

(b) There is a single, well-defined decision point (preoperative preparation for a case) when a number of important, related decisions must be made as to how best to handle the different phases of anesthetic management.

(c) The alternatives are sufficiently constrained to be manageable, but varied enough to be interesting.

(d) There are well-defined risks and benefits in the presence of certain diseases, and interesting risk tradeoffs in complicated patients.

As a result, anesthesia provides a fertile test ground for exploring computer-assisted management and for exploring ATTENDING's critiquing approach.

3 The ATTENDING system: overview

3.1 ANESTHESIOLOGY AND ANESTHETIC MANAGEMENT

Anesthesiology is a field which had its beginnings over a century ago, with the historic first public demonstration of ether anesthesia in 1846 at the Massachusetts General Hospital by Dr. William Morton, a dentist. For many years, ether was the mainstay of anesthetic practice. Particularly in the past fifty years, however, a wide range of different techniques and agents have come into use.

Throughout its history, anesthesiology has had to pay particular attention to risk. In the past there have been significant risks involved in the anesthetic agents themselves. For instance, ether and cyclopropane are two anesthetic gases in wide use as recently as the 1960's. Both agents are explosive. Furthermore when these agents are inhaled, they must, of course, be mixed with oxygen, usually enriched oxygen. All that is required to ignite the mixture is a spark. The patient's lungs might then explode.

Fortunately the anesthetic agents used today are very safe if used properly. They are not explosive. The anesthetic risks for a healthy, normal individual are very low, roughly equivalent to those of riding in a car.

With the advent of safe anesthetic agents, and with the recent development of sophisticated hemodynamic monitoring equipment and respiratory support, the character of anesthetic practice has greatly changed. Over the past two decades, there has been a trend towards much sicker patients being brought to surgery.

This trend has coincided with the great increase in cardiac surgery which has occurred over the past fifteen years. The management of cardiac cases has given anesthetists a great deal of experience with unstable patients, and has helped spur the development of the sophisticated technology that makes the care of such patients feasible.

As a result, whereas 30 or 40 years ago an elderly patient with minor or moderate medical problems would not have been considered an appropriate anesthetic risk, today the delivery of anesthesia to such a patient is routine. In fact, much sicker patients, including patients with multi-organ failure who are virtually at death's door, not infrequently come for surgery.

Modern anesthesia is still a high risk specialty but the risks today have a much different character than in the past. Morbidity and mortality can still result from human error, and from uncommon reactions to drugs, but these are rare. The dominant risks today stem from the preexisting disease (including heart, kidney, pulmonary, and neurologic disease) which patients bring with them to the operating room. Anesthetic management must be tailored to try to minimize these risks. This is the process which anesthetic decision-making centers around, and which the ATTENDING system is designed to critique.

3.1.1 Components of anesthetic management

In planning a patient's anesthetic management, a number of related decisions must be made. First one must decide whether to give general anesthesia (put the patient to sleep) or a regional technique (numb a region of the body such as an arm, a leg, or the lower extremities). One must then decide which specific drugs and techniques will be used. For instance, for general anesthesia, one must decide how to <u>induce</u> anesthesia (initially put the patient off to sleep), whether and how to <u>intubate</u> the patient (insert a breathing tube), and how to <u>maintain</u> anesthesia (keep the patient asleep). There are a number of different drugs and techniques available for each of these stages of anesthetic management. Each drug and each technique has its own set of risks and benefits in certain patients.

3.2 AN EXAMPLE

To use ATTENDING, an anesthetist first evaluates a patient scheduled for surgery, and formulates a tentative plan for that patient's management. He then inputs to ATTENDING:

(a) a list of the patient's underlying medical problems,

(b) the planned surgical procedure,

(c) an anesthetic plan specifying the agents and techniques to be used for premedication, induction, intubation, and maintenance of general or regional anesthesia.

ATTENDING critiques the plan from the perspective of the patient's underlying problems and their implied risks. In so doing, it discusses the risks and benefits of the proposed approach and of any reasonable alternatives. In this way, ATTENDING is designed to serve as a source of feedback to help the physician evaluate and optimize his approach.

3.2.1 Two modes of use

ATTENDING can be used in two modes: a consultation mode and a tutorial mode. In the consultation mode, as outlined above, the physician describes an actual patient by listing that patient's medical problems. Since the number of such problems in ATTENDING's present knowledge base is modest, the consultation mode's utility is currently limited.

In its tutorial mode, ATTENDING describes a hypothetical case to an anesthetist who then proposes a plan for the system to critique. In this mode, ATTENDING can be used for teaching while its data base is still small, since it need only know the anesthetic implications of those medical problems contained in the hypothetical cases. The tutorial mode allows anesthetist self-evaluation.

The only internal difference between the two modes is that in the consultation mode, the physician lists the patient's problems and the planned surgical procedure in addition to his proposed plan. In the tutorial mode this information is already known to the computer.

3.2.2 A hypothetical case

The following example illustrates the teaching use of the system. ATTENDING starts by describing a hypothetical case:

> A SIXTY YEAR OLD MAN, WITH A LONGSTANDING HISTORY OF CHRONIC RENAL FAILURE AND A PRIOR STROKE, COMES TO SURGERY FOR REMOVAL OF A METAL SPLINTER EMBEDDED IN HIS RIGHT EYE. HE RECENTLY ATE LUNCH.

This case involves a patient with four underlying medical problems: 1) chronic renal failure, 2) a prior stroke, 3) a penetrating eye wound, and 4) a full stomach. Each of these problems implies certain risks for the

27

patient's anesthetic management. A given anesthetic technique may increase these risks or may decrease them. In a complicated case with several medical problems, there are frequently risk tradeoffs. Techniques which are good for one problem are bad for another, and vice versa. As a result, an anesthetist must weigh these risks against one another, and in so doing, tailor a plan of management to the patient's underlying problems and their implied risks.

The major risk tradeoffs in this example revolve around the question of how best to intubate the patient (pass a breathing tube into his trachea to secure and protect his airway). There are a number of possible approaches which could be taken. Each involves some risk, as is outlined below:

No intubation Since the patient has a full stomach, no intubation involves the risk that his stomach contents might be regurgitated and aspirated into his lungs. This is frequently fatal.

Awake intubation Intubating the patient while still awake is perhaps the safest way to avoid aspiration but can be very uncomfortable for the patient and is therefore seldom done unless there is a specific indication. In a patient with a penetrating eye wound, awake intubation also involves the risk of loss of the eye, since coughing and straining may occur which can cause increased intraocular pressure.

Rapid-sequence intubation using succinylcholine Rapid-sequence intubation is a technique for expeditiously intubating a patient with a full stomach immediately after induction of anesthesia. For this purpose, the fast acting muscle relaxant, succinylcholine, is frequently used. In this patient, however, use of succinylcholine involves 1) the risk of loss of the eye since succinylcholine can increase intraocular pressure, and 2) the risk of life-threatening hyperkalemia, if the prior stroke was recent and involved hemiparesis.

Rapid-sequence intubation using high dose pancuronium An alternative method of performing rapid-sequence intubation is to use a different muscle relaxant, such as pancuronium. A high dose must be used since otherwise the onset of action is too slow. In a patient with renal disease, however, this approach involves the risk of postoperative paralysis due to compromised renal excretion of the pancuronium.

<u>Intubation after mask induction with cricoid pressure</u> A further alternative is to induce anesthesia in a "non-rapid" fashion, using pressure on the cricoid cartilage (in the neck) to help prevent regurgitation of stomach contents up the esophagus. This technique does involve a certain increased risk of aspiration, although much less than with no intubation.

A physician outlines his plan by specifying his choices from a "menu" of alternatives. This process takes a minute or two. Shown below is a plan which might be proposed for the example patient:

<pre>
                 INDUCTION: THIOPENTAL
PLAN 1:   INTUBATION: RAPID-SEQUENCE SUCCINYLCHOLINE
                 MAINTENANCE: HALOTHANE CURARE N2O O2
</pre>

This plan proposes <u>induction</u> of general anesthesia with thiopental (a short-acting barbiturate), rapid-sequence <u>intubation</u> using succinylcholine (a rapid-acting, short-acting muscle relaxant), and <u>maintenance</u> of anesthesia with halothane (an inhalational anesthetic), curare (a long-acting muscle relaxant), nitrous oxide, and oxygen. ATTENDING currently produces the following critique of this plan:

THERE ARE A NUMBER OF BASIC PRINCIPLES INVOLVED IN THIS PATIENT'S MANAGEMENT. FIRST, A PATIENT WITH CHRONIC RENAL FAILURE MUST BE PROTECTED FROM RENAL TOXICITY AND COMPROMISED RENAL EXCRETION OF DRUGS. SECOND, IN A PATIENT WITH A PRIOR STROKE, ONE MUST CONSIDER THE PROBLEM OF HYPERKALEMIA. THIRD, IN THE PRESENCE OF A PENETRATING EYE WOUND, ONE MUST ATTEMPT TO PREVENT EYE MORBIDITY. ALSO, A PATIENT WITH A FULL STOMACH MUST BE PROTECTED FROM ASPIRATION.

INTUBATION OF THIS PATIENT IS CLEARLY IMPORTANT BECAUSE OF A FULL STOMACH. RAPID SEQUENCE INTUBATION IS A REASONABLE APPROACH. THE CHOICE OF SUCCINYLCHOLINE, HOWEVER, COULD HAVE TWO POSSIBLE RISKS. FIRST, IN A PATIENT WITH A PENETRATING EYE WOUND, THERE IS THE RISK OF EYE MORBIDITY

FROM INCREASED INTRAOCULAR PRESSURE. SECOND, IF THE STROKE IS RECENT AND INVOLVES HEMIPARESIS, THERE IS THE RISK OF LIFE-THREATENING HYPERKALEMIA. AN ALTERNATIVE WOULD BE HIGH DOSE PANCURONIUM. HERE, HOWEVER, THERE IS THE RISK THAT THIS COULD CAUSE PROLONGED POSTOPERATIVE PARALYSIS DUE TO COMPROMISED RENAL EXCRETION. THUS, THERE IS NO IDEAL WAY TO PERFORM RAPID SEQUENCE INTUBATION. AN ALTERNATIVE APPROACH, PERHAPS, TO RAPID SEQUENCE INTUBATION WOULD BE INTUBATION AFTER MASK INDUCTION WITH CRICOID PRESSURE.

LOOKING AT OTHER ASPECTS OF THE PROPOSED PLAN, FOR A PATIENT WITH CHRONIC RENAL FAILURE, CURARE IS A REASONABLE SELECTION SINCE IT IS RELIABLY METABOLIZED BY THE LIVER, AND HALOTHANE IS A GOOD CHOICE SINCE IT HAS NO NEPHROTOXICITY.

A number of features of this critique merit discussion:

The initial discussion of underlying principles The first paragraph of the critique discusses the underlying principles involved in the patient's anesthetic management. This introductory discussion is currently somewhat rudimentary, but serves to set the tone for the critique itself which follows.

The body of the critique Next, the management plan itself is analyzed. This is the heart of the critique. Since the major risks in this patient involve intubation, the critique centers on this aspect of the plan. In the analysis, the system mentions positive aspects of the plan along with any criticisms, on the theory that advice is best received when presented in as positive a context as possible. The final paragraph mentions two aspects of the plan which the system approves of.

The critique is not generated from stored paragraphs As described in detail in Chapter 6, this critique is not generated from stored paragraphs. Rather it is pieced together from words and sentence fragments, tailored to the particular approach to the particular patient's care.

The clinical goals of the critique The tutorial goal of the critique is to let the physician exercise his intellectual anesthetic management skills and get feedback. When used for consultation, the goal is to make sure the physician has fully thought through the patient's problems and their management implications, after which the physician is, of course, free to do as he pleases.

3.2.3 Three further critiques

To illustrate ATTENDING's approach more fully, the remainder of this section shows how ATTENDING critiques other plans involving the same patient described above. In the following example, for instance, instead of using succinylcholine (which involves major risks), the anesthetist has proposed rapid-sequence intubation with high-dose pancuronium. (To avoid repetition in the critiques that follow, the initial paragraph discussing management principles is omitted. Since the same patient is being discussed, it would be unchanged.)

INDUCTION: THIOPENTAL
PLAN 2:   INTUBATION: RAPID-SEQUENCE PANCURONIUM
MAINTENANCE: HALOTHANE PANCURONIUM N20 02

INTUBATION OF THIS PATIENT IS CERTAINLY NECESSARY BECAUSE OF A FULL STOMACH. RAPID SEQUENCE INTUBATION IS A REASONABLE APPROACH. THE CHOICE OF HIGH DOSE PANCURONIUM, HOWEVER, INVOLVES THE RISK OF PROLONGED POSTOPERATIVE PARALYSIS DUE TO COMPROMISED RENAL EXCRETION. AN ALTERNATIVE APPROACH, PERHAPS, TO RAPID SEQUENCE INTUBATION WOULD BE INTUBATION AFTER MASK INDUCTION WITH CRICOID PRESSURE.

LOOKING AT OTHER ASPECTS OF THE PROPOSED PLAN, FOR A PATIENT WITH CHRONIC RENAL FAILURE, HALOTHANE IS A GOOD CHOICE SINCE IT HAS NO NEPHROTOXICITY.

Here the paragraph discussing intubation is shorter because the use of succinylcholine need not be discussed (since it involves higher potential risk than the chosen approach). Indeed, in each of these example critiques, several conceivable (but inferior) approaches to intubation are not mentioned at all: including no intubation, awake intubation, etc. As described in Chapter 5, in its internal analysis ATTENDING weighs the various risks involved, and thereby focuses its discussion on the clinically relevant choices.

Plan 3, below, is identical to Plan 2 except that here induction is proposed using ketamine, a drug which has risks in the presence of a penetrating eye wound. As a result, a paragraph discussing induction is added. (Induction was not discussed in the previous two critiques since the proposed approach to induction was reasonable.)

	INDUCTION: KETAMINE
PLAN 3:	INTUBATION: RAPID-SEQUENCE PANCURONIUM
	MAINTENANCE: HALOTHANE PANCURONIUM N20 02

INTUBATION OF THIS PATIENT IS DEFINITELY APPROPRIATE BECAUSE OF A FULL STOMACH. RAPID SEQUENCE INTUBATION IS A REASONABLE APPROACH. THE CHOICE OF HIGH DOSE PANCURONIUM, HOWEVER, MIGHT HAVE THE RISK OF PROLONGED POSTOPERATIVE PARALYSIS DUE TO COMPROMISED RENAL EXCRETION. AN ALTERNATIVE APPROACH, PERHAPS, TO RAPID SEQUENCE INTUBATION WOULD BE INTUBATION AFTER MASK INDUCTION WITH CRICOID PRESSURE.

FROM THE STANDPOINT OF INDUCTION, INDUCTION WITH KETAMINE INVOLVES THE RISK OF EYE MORBIDITY FROM INCREASED INTRAOCULAR PRESSURE. AN ALTERNATIVE APPROACH TO INDUCTION WITH KETAMINE WOULD BE INDUCTION USING THIOPENTAL.

LOOKING AT OTHER ASPECTS OF THE PROPOSED PLAN, FOR A PATIENT WITH CHRONIC RENAL FAILURE, HALOTHANE IS A GOOD CHOICE SINCE IT HAS NO NEPHROTOXOCITY.

Finally, Plan 4 shows how ATTENDING responds if no intubation is proposed:

	INDUCTION: THIOPENTAL
PLAN 4:	INTUBATION: NONE
	MAINTENANCE: HALOTHANE CURARE N20 02

ALTHOUGH INTUBATION OF THIS PATIENT WAS NOT PROPOSED, IT IS CLEARLY DESIRABLE. NOT INTUBATING THIS PATIENT WOULD HAVE THE RISK OF ASPIRATION.

LOOKING AT OTHER ASPECTS OF THE PROPOSED PLAN, FOR A PATIENT WITH CHRONIC RENAL FAILURE, CURARE IS A REASONABLE SELECTION SINCE IT IS

RELIABLY METABOLIZED BY THE LIVER, AND HALOTHANE IS A GOOD CHOICE SINCE IT HAS NO NEPHROTOXICITY.

Notice that ATTENDING mentions why intubation should be performed, but does not discuss which technique might be preferred. The physician could obtain such a critique by submitting an amended plan containing a proposed intubation technique.

Further example critiques can be seen in Appendix I. As these examples illustrate, ATTENDING must do more than just propose a reasonable approach to a patient's management and justify its choice. To critique a plan effectively, it must be prepared to handle any approach (good, marginal, or poor) and still produce an intelligent, focused critique. The following chapters discuss how the system is designed to achieve this capability.

3.3 AN OVERVIEW OF ATTENDING'S SYSTEM DESIGN

Before ATTENDING's implementation is described in detail, this section gives an overview of two aspects of the system's design: 1) how it represents its medical knowledge, and 2) its sequence of operation.

3.3.1 ATTENDING's medical knowledge

In analyzing an anesthetic plan, ATTENDING must weigh the risks and benefits of alternative approaches to the patient's management. As discussed above, these risks and benefits are determined by the patient's underlying problems.

Figure 3.1 outlines how this knowledge is organized internally in ATTENDING. (The details of this knowledge are discussed later.) The knowledge of alternative anesthetic techniques is stored in the form of Augmented Decision Networks (ADNs). As described in Chapter 4, the arcs of these networks explicitly spell out the various decisions and subdecisions that make up an anesthetic plan.

The knowledge of the anesthetic implications of a patient's underlying medical problems is stored in Problem Management Frames. Each problem (e.g. asthma, coronary artery disease, renal failure) has an associated frame, which describes how that problem influences anesthetic management decisions. In particular, each frame lists a set of management principles,

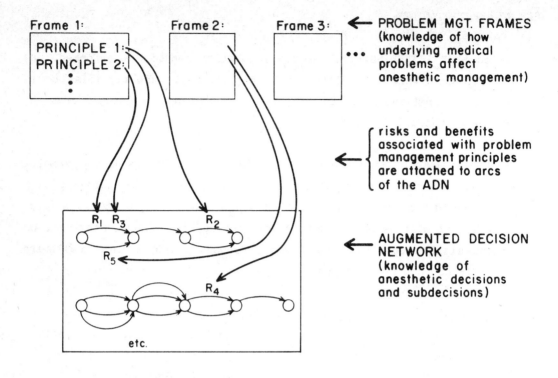

Figure 3.1   An outline of ATTENDING's medical knowledge.
(Miller 1983a, ©1983 IEEE)

Figure 3.2   ATTENDING's sequence of operation.
(Miller 1983a, ©1983 IEEE)

plus a list of risks and benefits. These risks and benefits are also in turn attached to ADN arcs. In this way, each problem management frame indicates which techniques are to be avoided or preferred in the presence of that medical problem. Similarly, each anesthetic technique (ADN arc) has a list of all the risks and benefits associated with that technique in the presence of different underlying medical problems.

3.3.2 ATTENDING's sequence of operation

The process ATTENDING goes through in analyzing a physician's plan is outlined in Figure 3.2. First, a <u>conversion routine</u> transforms the physician's plan, expressed as "menu selections", into a tree-structured form called here the Proposed Approach Tree (PAT). The PAT is then passed to the <u>ADN Analyzer</u> which uses the Augmented Decision Networks, together with the risks and benefits which augment their arcs, to analyze the proposed approach. This analysis produces the Alternative Tree (AT), which includes the proposed approach plus any alternatives which ATTENDING has found. Finally, the AT is input to the <u>Prose Generator</u> which produces the prose analysis.

The next three chapters discuss these components of the ATTENDING system in detail. In particular, they describe in turn how three central problems are addressed:

(a) <u>The exploration of alternatives</u> ATTENDING must be able to explore flexibly all possible approaches to a patient's management.

(b) <u>Risk analysis</u> It must be able to compare the risks of alternative approaches in an intelligent, focused way.

(c) <u>Prose generation</u> It must be able to generate a potentially complex prose analysis which critiques the plan in a readable, easily understood form.

4 Exploring alternative approaches

This chapter describes how ATTENDING is designed to explore alternative approaches to a patient's anesthetic management. To allow this, the physician's plan is first converted to a tree-structured form, the "Proposed Approach Tree" (PAT). Figure 4.1 shows the PAT constructed from the first example plan. This tree explicitly outlines the hierarchy of decisions and subdecisions which the physician has made in formulating the plan. Thus, this initial routine converts the plan from the "menu selection" format in which the anesthetist expresses it, into a tree-structured form which serves as input to ATTENDING's further analysis.

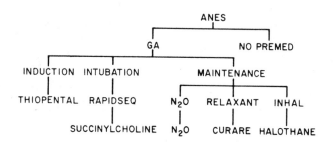

Figure 4.1 The Proposed Approach Tree (PAT)
(Miller 1983a, © 1983 IEEE)

4.1 THE AUGMENTED DECISION NETWORK (ADN)

ATTENDING uses "Augmented Decision Networks" (ADNs) to guide its exploration of the alternatives involved in anesthetic management. ATTENDING's ADNs are based on the "Augmented Transition Network" (ATN)

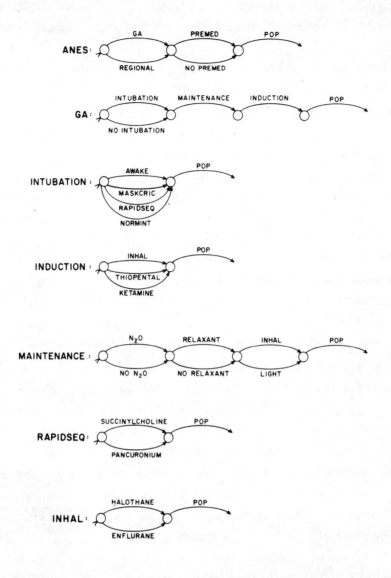

Figure 4.2 Several augmented decision networks used by ATTENDING.
(Miller 1983a, © 1983 IEEE)

formalism which has been widely used in natural language and speech understanding systems (Woods 1970). The ATN affords ATTENDING an easily understood, hierarchical formalism for the representation of anesthetic plans.

Several ADNs currently used by ATTENDING are shown in Figure 4.2. Each ADN is composed of states (represented by circles) connected by arcs. Each network has an initial state. Starting from this initial state, one follows successive arcs, tracing a path through the network. If an arc labelled POP is chosen, it represents the end of the path in that network.

Each arc is either a terminal or a non-terminal arc. A terminal arc is labelled with the name of a drug (curare, halothane, etc.) or an "elemental" technique (such as nasal intubation). Each non-terminal arc is labelled by the name of a "non-elemental" technique (such as general anesthesia, intubation, or induction). These are "non-elemental" in the sense that further sub-decisions must be made to completely specify how the technique is to be implemented.

When following a path through a network, whenever a non-terminal arc is encountered, one must find the subnetwork which defines the technique named and trace a path through that network before continuing the path in the original network. This process is called "pushing" to the "lower" network. "Popping" is the process of returning to the original "higher" network from which one has pushed. (This terminology is well established in computational linguistics in connection with ATN grammars.)

As can be seen, it is possible to push to several successively lower networks before eventually popping back up the successive levels to the original network. This corresponds to the process of making subdecisions within subdecisions within subdecisions, etc.

For example, the highest level network is labelled ANES (anesthesia). Two possible arcs lead from its initial state: labelled GA (general anesthesia), and REGIONAL (regional anesthesia). If the GA arc is chosen, then before traversing it, one must first go to the network named GA and choose a path through it. In the process of choosing this path, additional lower level networks must, in turn, be explored.

Each network, then, represents a set of related decisions, and the lower networks represent subdecisions which must be made to fully define a decision made in a higher network. In this way, the ADN is able to

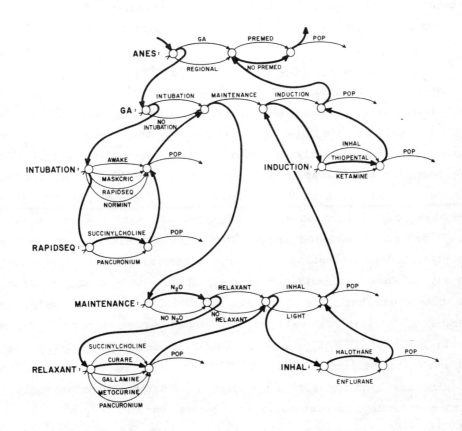

Figure 4.3 The complete path which corresponds to the example PAT.
(Miller 1983a, ©1983 IEEE)

structure the hierarchical decisions that go into formulating anesthetic management in a natural way. A path through the entire set of networks corresponds to a complete anesthetic plan. Figure 4.3 shows the path which represents the first example plan from Chapter 3.

Section 4.2 describes how ADNs are used to explore alternative approaches to the physician's plan. The remainder of this subsection discusses four issues to help put the ADN into perspective.

4.1.1 The ADN vs. other hierarchical planning structures

The ADN is a hierarchical decision formalism which is well suited to the type of anesthetic management plans critiqued by ATTENDING. Several previous research projects have addressed the analysis of computer programs, which are highly stylized plans to accomplish a task (Sussman 1975; M Miller and Goldstein 1977; Rich et al. 1979). Other hierarchical planning structures, as in NOAH (Sacerdoti 1977) and MOLGEN (Stefik 1981), have been developed to handle other types of plans. A particular issue which these have addressed is the fact that subdecisions are not always completely independent of one another. Subdecisions made in one part of a plan may influence subdecisions made elsewhere. Only a single instance of this phenomenon has been found in ATTENDING's domain: namely, in the presence of certain medical problems (such as an upper airway mass), certain risks of induction are no longer present if intubation has been done with the patient awake. ATTENDING's ADNs do not have a general mechanism for handling such subproblem interactions. Rather this single instance is handled heuristically as a special case.

A positive feature of the ADN formalism is that it is easily understood. An anesthetist can look at Figure 4.3 and relate to it readily.

4.1.2 The ADN vs. a decision tree

The ADN also has the advantage of being similar to the decision tree: a formalism which has been extensively used in clinical decision analysis (Weinstein 1980). In a typical clinical decision tree, paths from an initial state successively diverge. The ADN differs in that paths which diverge at one point may later rejoin. This allows much greater economy of expression in defining decisions to be made. For instance, in the MAINTENANCE network (Figure 4.2), whether or not N_2O is used, one must still decide whether to use a muscle relaxant, and then one must choose a basic anesthetic technique. Were the network paths not allowed to rejoin, the number of states and arcs would proliferate exponentially as each possible combination was represented by a separate path.

A second way in which an ADN differs from a decision tree is in its hierachical nature: allowing subdecisions to be represented by separate "lower" networks. As mentioned previously, this allows the hierarchical structure of anesthetic decision-making to be captured naturally.

4.1.3 Is the full power of the ADN needed?

Although the ADN formalism allows for complex interconnections of arcs and states, the current ADNs used by ATTENDING (Figure 4.2) have been deliberately restricted. Each network can be seen to be a linear sequence of states, with the arcs leaving a given state all going to a single next state. As a result, each network could be converted to a simpler formalism involving ANDs, and ORs, as depicted in Figure 4.4.

If, in the long run, this restriction still allows the type of decision-making involved in anesthetic management to be efficiently expressed, then perhaps the full ADN formalism is unnecessary. On the other hand, as discussed in section 4.1.1, a more powerful planning formalism may ultimately prove necessary to handle such problems as interacting subplans. This question remains to be answered.

4.1.4 In what way is an ADN "augmented"?

An ADN is augmented in two ways. 1) As mentioned previously in Chapter 3, each arc of an ADN has an associated list of risks and benefits that help guide the analysis of alternative approaches. 2) As in an ATN grammar, each arc of an ADN has an associated "action routine". An action routine is a LISP procedure which can set and test contextual flags to guide the exploration of the ADN. This facility allows contextual constraints to be incorporated into an ADN. For example, it makes no sense to consider spinal anesthesia for an eye operation. Therefore, in critiquing a plan involving eye surgery, the arc representing spinal anesthesia is inactivated. This is done by the action routine associated with that arc.

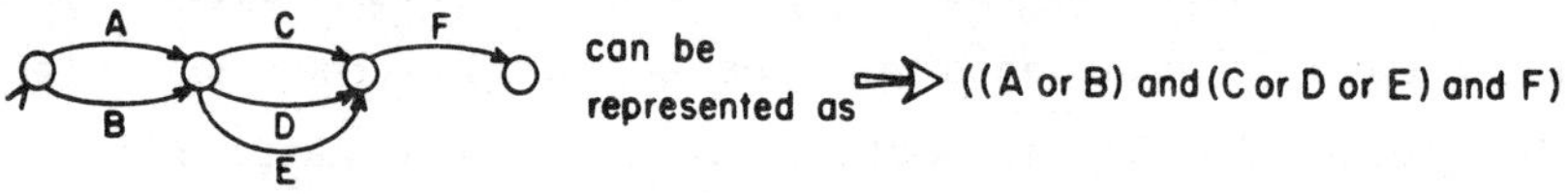

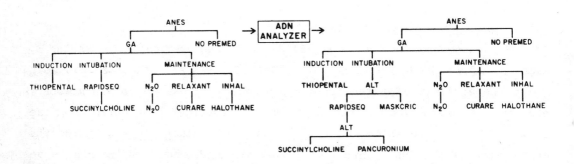

A → B → C → D → E → F   can be represented as ⟹ ((A or B) and (C or D or E) and F)

Figure 4.4 The current simplified ADNs could be represented
by ORs and ANDs. (Miller 1983a, ©1983 IEEE)

Figure 4.5 Creation of the AT by the ADN analyzer.
(Miller 1983a, ©1983 IEEE)

4.2 THE ANALYSIS OF ALTERNATIVE APPROACHES

As the ATTENDING system analyzes the PAT using the ADNs, it constructs an
<u>Alternative Tree</u> (AT), as illustrated in Figure 4.5. The AT is very
similar to the PAT. There are two main differences. First, each node of
the AT has an associated list which specifies the risks and benefits of
using that technique with the given patient. Second, the AT may, at any
level, contain alternative approaches to be considered. Thus, in Figure
4.5, an alternative approach to succinylcholine is indicated, as well as an
alternative approach to rapid-sequence intubation.

The AT is constructed by tracing alternative paths through the ADNs,
starting with the topmost network (ANES), as follows:

(a) At each state, ATTENDING first checks to see which, if any, arc (arc A)
    was chosen by the physician: i.e. which technique was indicated in the
    PAT.

(b) ATTENDING then evaluates the risk associated with arc A. If arc A is a
    terminal arc, this can be done merely by examining risk definitions
    augmenting the arc. If arc A is a non-terminal arc, however, then to
    evaluate its risk, ATTENDING must <u>push</u> to the first state of the
    apppropriate lower network and evaluate its risk, before it can <u>pop</u>
    back to arc A. (The approach used to evaluate and compare risks is
    described in Chapter 5.)

(c) Once the risk of arc A is determined, ATTENDING evaluates the risk of
    all alternative arcs. Any whose risk is equal or less than that of arc
    A is incorporated into the AT as a possible alternative approach. (If
    arc A has <u>no risk</u>, however, only alternative arcs with benefits are
    incorporated into the AT.)

By structuring decisions hierarchically and exploring them as described
above, ATTENDING first considers alternatives that involve the smallest
global change. For instance, if the physician proposes using halothane (an
inhalational anesthetic) and if this involves some risk, then in processing
the ADNs, ATTENDING first looks to see if another inhalational anesthetic
involves no risk or less risk. Only if all inhalational anesthetics

involve risk, does ATTENDING consider other approaches to general anesthesia, and only if these all involve risk, does it consider more global alternatives such as a regional technique. This feature, which is implicit in the design, helps the system tailor its advice to the physician's plan in a natural way.

5 A heuristic approach to risk analysis

To evaluate a physician's plan intelligently, ATTENDING must do more than merely explore the various alternative approaches. To be effective, it must then be able to assess the relative merits of the different approaches, and to discuss any risks and benefits in an appropriate way.

This section describes the heuristic approach to risk analysis which ATTENDING has taken. This approach involves three basic principles, each of which is discussed in detail. Before discussing how the ATTENDING system handles risk, however, let us briefly consider a more conventional approach to risk.

5.1 CONVENTIONAL RISK ANALYSIS

The conventional approach to risk analysis, as used in economic cost/benefit analysis and clinical decision analysis (Weinstein 1980), attempts to reduce the risks involved in decision-making to <u>numbers</u> to allow precise comparison. This analysis typically consists of the following steps for each choice in the decision-making process:

(a) defining all possible <u>outcomes</u> i,
(b) assigning some <u>value</u> (V_i) to each outcome,
(c) determining a <u>likelihood</u> (L_i) for each outcome,
(d) computing an "expected value" for that choice, by summing $L_i * V_i$.

The difficulties inherent in this general approach are well recognized, both in medicine and in many other areas where cost/benefit analysis has been applied. First of all, it is hard to assign precise values to many outcomes, for instance: loss of life, loss of a limb or an eye, bronchospasm, hypotension, and other medical complications of varying severity. Also, the likelihoods of the various risks are not easy to determine precisely. Different studies often produce quite different figures. Furthermore, it is often hard to know how a reported complication rate applies to a given patient with a particular set of medical problems.

Finally, the only way to gather many statistics would be to deliberately manage a group of patients poorly and document the bad results that occurred: a clearly impractical project.

Such numerical risk analysis is certainly important in trying to make real-world decisions as rational as possible, which is the goal of clinical decision analysis and cost/benefit analysis. It is unclear, however, that a system like ATTENDING must take this approach. ATTENDING's goal is not to quantify the risks of the various alternatives, but rather to lay out the reasonable alternatives, and let the physician use his experience and judgement to make the final decisions.

If ATTENDING were to adopt the numerical approach, massive data gathering would be required, and much of it would be impossible to obtain. Also, granting the uncertainties discussed above, it would be difficult to take the data and add, multiply, and otherwise manipulate it, and still have a good feeling for the exact meaning of the result.

A system which used this numerical approach might produce a ranked list of alternatives, with each choice having an associated score indicating how "good" that choice was. The user might well be baffled as to how to interpret each score, and by what to make of a particular difference between two scores.

In contrast to this conventional, numerical approach to risk analysis, a physician deals with problems of medical management every day with only an approximate feel for the magnitudes of the various risks involved. Instead, he takes a <u>heuristic approach</u> to risk analysis, as indeed do people in general in their everyday lives. Certainly it is useful to try to define all the various risk parameters as accurately as possible, as done in clinical decision analysis. At the same time, however, it is equally worthwhile to work on incorporating a more heuristic approach to risk analysis into the machine. The current implementation of the ATTENDING system is a step in this direction.

5.2 <u>THREE PRINCIPLES FOR HEURISTIC RISK ANALYSIS</u>

Instead of reducing the risks of various alternatives to numbers to allow precise comparison, the ATTENDING system bases its approach to risk on the following <u>three principles</u>:

I.   Rough general criteria are used to eliminate obviously poor choices.

II.   Domain-specific knowledge is used to focus attention on the most clinically appropriate alternatives.

III.   The relevant risks and benefits are then discussed in a pertinent, natural way.

Figure 5.1 illustrates the application of these three principles. Here, starting with five possible alternative approaches (A-E), Principle I is first applied to eliminate two obviously poor choices, B and E. Next, using Principle II, attention is focused on two of the remaining choices, A and D. The risks and benefits of these are then discussed (Principle III) with the physician, who makes the final choice.

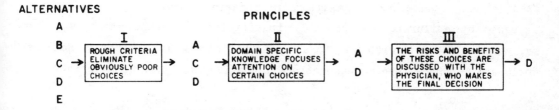

Figure 5.1 The application of the three principles.
(Miller 1983a, © 1983 IEEE)

This selection process is applied at each level of decision and sub-decision in analyzing a plan. The remainder of this section discusses these three principles in turn, and describes specifically how ATTENDING implements each.

Principle 1: Rough criteria eliminate obviously poor choices
If one outlines all possible ways to accomplish a task, there are

frequently choices which are clearly inferior. When a person is the decision-maker, many of these poor choices may not even come to mind. They are weeded out at an unconscious level. When a machine is evaluating the alternatives, however, any selection capability of this sort must be explicitly built in.

The use of rough estimates of the "magnitude" of a risk allows ATTENDING to achieve this type of "broadbrush" selection capability. For this purpose, each risk is assigned a rough magnitude: LOW, MODERATE, HIGH, or EXTREME. Thus, just as the computerized diagnostic systems described in (Szolovits 1982, Clancey and Shortliffe 1983) use rough estimates of diagnostic likelihood to drive their analyses (Szolovits and Pauker 1978), ATTENDING uses rough estimates of risk.

Several concrete examples may help illustrate how these risk magnitudes are assigned:

Low magnitude An example of a LOW magnitude anesthetic risk is that of using enflurane, an inhalational anesthetic, when a patient has renal failure (RF). Enflurane releases fluoride ion metabolites, which could theoretically cause renal damage. In practice, however, the quantities released by enflurane are probably insufficient to cause problems. Even so, for a patient with RF, most anesthetists would probably not use enflurane if there were a reasonable alternative, as there usually is.

Extreme magnitude An example of an EXTREME magnitude is the risk that a patient with a full stomach might aspirate (regurgitate and inhale his stomach contents), if his airway is not protected with an endotracheal tube. Aspiration is frequently fatal.

High magnitude An example of a HIGH magnitude is the risk of using succinylcholine in a patient with a penetrating eye wound. Succinylcholine increases intracocular pressure and could thereby lead to loss of the eye.

In addition to risks, management choices may also involve benefits. In ATTENDING, benefits too are characterized by a rough magnitude, and are treated internally as "negative risks". In the domain of anesthesia, benefits seem to fall mostly in the LOW to MODERATE range. An example is the advantage (benefit) of inducing anesthesia with ketamine when a patient has asthma, since ketamine is a bronchodilator.

Formally, the "magnitude" of a risk, as used in ATTENDING, corresponds to a rough estimate of its "expected value": its likelihood multiplied by the value of its outcome (i.e. a rough estimate of $L_i * V_i$). Clinically, these risk magnitudes seem to conform naturally to the way an anesthetist thinks about risks, and are therefore quite easy to assign.

When manipulating risk magnitudes internally, ATTENDING makes certain simplifications for the purpose of broadbrush comparison. If a choice incurs several risks, the risk magnitudes are not added together to determine the total risk magnitude of that choice. Rather, the largest risk magnitude is used. Thus if a given choice involves one LOW risk and two MODERATE risks, the total risk magnitude assigned to that choice is MODERATE. (All three risks, of course, might be mentioned in the eventual prose analysis.)

Therefore, even though there might be several risks and sub-risks involved in a choice being evaluated, that choice is always characterized by a single risk magnitude. As a result of this simplification, rough general comparison between two choices is very straightforward. If the risk magnitudes are not the same, then one choice is clearly inferior and can be discarded. The only exception is that the physician's choice is always retained, even if it is inferior, since it will serve as a basis for the later critique.

Thus, if four alternative choices exist, two with LOW risk, one with MODERATE risk, and one with HIGH risk, the MODERATE and the HIGH risk choices can be discarded, leaving only the two LOW risk choices for further analysis. For instance, in the first example critique, the possibility of not intubating the patient (which has the EXTREME risk of aspiration) is discarded early in ATTENDING'S analysis and never mentioned in the critique.

Principle 2: Domain-specific knowledge focuses attention on the most clinically appropriate alternatives

Using rough estimates of risk as discussed above, ATTENDING is able to discard obviously poor choices, and is left with alternative choices which have risks of equal "rough magnitude". This broadbrush discrimination, however, may not be sufficient to let the system focus on the most clinically appropriate alternatives for discussion with the physician. More specific knowledge may have to be brought to bear.

To allow this more selective focusing of ATTENDING's attention on the clinically most appropriate alternatives, the ATTENDING system uses "Contextual Preference Rules" (CP rules). CP rules are designed to let the system look at approaches which have the same risk magnitude (LOW, MODERATE, etc.) and selectively focus on a preferred approach in a given context. Each CP rule has four parts, which respectively state that 1) in the context of a particular medical problem, 2) a certain specified technique is most likely preferable to 3) another specified technique. The CP rule also states 4) the reason for the preference.

For instance, in the current ATTENDING implementation, there is a CP rule stating that 1) in the presence of coronary artery disease, 2) intubation after mask induction with cricoid pressure may be preferable to 3) rapid sequence intubation because 4) it allows more gradual induction with less danger of sudden cardiac decompensation. In the following paragraph, one can observe this CP rule being used in discussing a plan.

INTUBATION OF THIS PATIENT IS DEFINITELY APPROPRIATE BECAUSE OF A FULL STOMACH. RAPID SEQUENCE INTUBATION IS A REASONABLE APPROACH. THIS MIGHT HOWEVER, HAVE THE RISK OF CARDIAC COMPROMISE. AN ALTERNATIVE APPROACH TO RAPID SEQUENCE INTUBATION WOULD BE INTUBATION AFTER MASK INDUCTION WITH CRICOID PRESSURE. THIS HAS THE ADVANTAGE OF HELPING AVOID HYPOTENSION. INTUBATION AFTER MASK INDUCTION WITH CRICOID PRESSURE MIGHT WELL BE PREFERABLE FOR A PATIENT WITH CORONARY ARTERY DISEASE, IF SEVERE, SINCE IT ALLOWS MORE GRADUAL INDUCTION WITH LESS DANGER OF SUDDEN CARDIAC DECOMPENSATION.

The advantage of using CP rules is that not only can the system focus on a preferred approach, it can also justify its choice since it knows the reason for the preference. Thus, CP rules play two roles. First, they allow ATTENDING to focus selectively on certain approaches. Second, if the physician has proposed a "less preferred" choice, a CP rule gives ATTENDING a reason it can use in justifying its suggestion of the "more preferred" approach.

To understand the role played by these CP rules, it is instructive to discuss how their use differs from "fudging" (i.e. futher refining) the risk magnitudes. In other words, why have CP rules at all? Why not, for instance, in the presence of coronary artery disease, somehow adjust the risk magnitudes associated with "rapid sequence intubation" and "intubation after mask induction with cricoid pressure" so that they are no longer equal, and so that the latter is preferable, purely from the standpoint of risk magnitudes?

There are several disadvantages to such "fudging". First of all, once one starts systematically "fudging" risk magnitudes in this way, even the system designer can rapidly lose sight of the various permutations of exactly when and where one technique is preferable to another, and why. Equally important, by burying the preference information in these weighting factors, this information is irretrievably lost to the system itself. It can no longer explain and justify its preferences to its physician user.

Of course, one might argue that the use of CP rules has the practical effect of "fudging" the risk magnitudes, since the CP rules are superimposed upon the risk magnitude analysis and serve to refine it. Perhaps so, but by using CP rules, this is done explicitly. The risk magnitude analysis is kept simple and is easily understood. The CP rules themselves state clearly where and when they operate. And most important, as mentioned previously, they allow the system to explain and justify the preferences.

Principle 3: Discussion of relevant risks and benefits in a pertinent, natural way

The ability to discuss the relevant risks and benefits in a way that seems natural to the physician is of paramount importance. If the system cannot do this, then its impact will be greatly undermined. We have already shown how CP rules allow ATTENDING to explain certain of its recommendations to the physician. But more than this is needed. In particular, the system must tailor its discussion of each risk to the physician's own perception of that risk.

Risks have many facets. Not only do they have different magnitudes, they also have many other characteristic features. These features

influence how the physician thinks about each risk, and therefore how that
risk is best described. For instance, some risks are virtually certain,
and others are remote. Some are unanimously recognized, others are
controversial. Still others may be at best theoretical, and of little
practical importance. Some may be so obvious as to be implicit in any
discussion involving them.

These features might most aptly be called "pragmatic features" of
risks. Each risk has its own set of "pragmatic features". ATTENDING must
know about these pragmatic features if it is to discuss the risks
intelligently with the physician.

Among the pragmatic features used by ATTENDING to characterize risks are:

<u>Implicit</u> Some risks are implicit in the techniques being described. An
example is the risk of aspiration while doing a mask induction with cricoid
pressure for a patient with a full stomach. Another example is the cost
and risk implicit in preoperatively performing a tracheostomy to secure a
patient's airway. ATTENDING must know about these risks to be able to
evaluate alternative approaches to intubation. The system would sound
naive, however, if it discussed such implicit risks each time it mentioned
the technique involved. Thus, risks with the IMPLICIT feature are weighed
internally during ATTENDING's analysis, but are not mentioned to the
physician in the discussion of his plan.

<u>Theoretical</u> Some risks are really only of theoretical importance in that
they probably never cause major harm, even though they may often influence
a patient's management.   An example is the risk, discussed earlier, of
using enflurane in a patient with renal failure. Renal damage by enflurane
has never been documented. When these risks are discussed by ATTENDING,
they are couched in a phrase like, "there is <u>at least the theoretical risk
of</u> ---". This phrasing tailors the discussion to the physician's own
perception of that risk.

<u>Remote</u> Some risks, although acknowledged as real, may be perceived as
remote possibilities. An example is the risk of provoking bronchospasm by
inducing anesthesia with thiopental. It seldom actually happens.
ATTENDING's discussion of such a risk is couched in a phrase like,

"there is <u>the conceivable risk of</u> ---".

Pragmatic features such as these are necessary because the physician has different mental models of different risks. To discuss these risks with him in a natural way, wording must be chosen carefully to tailor the discussion to his mental models. If these pragmatic features are ignored, and ATTENDING discusses all risks in the same terms, then the system sounds like a school child reciting facts which it has memorized but does not fully understand.

If, on the other hand, the pragmatic features are used, and the discussion of each risk is appropriately modified or qualified, the anesthetist usually doesn't even notice that the discussion of different risks is being phrased differently.

5.3 <u>AN OVERVIEW OF ATTENDING'S APPROACH TO RISK</u>

This chapter has described the heuristic approach to risk analysis taken by ATTENDING. <u>Rather than characterize a risk by numbers representing its likelihood and morbidity, this approach characterizes a risk by a spectrum of attributes and knowledge, allowing a more robust evaluation and discussion of risk tradeoffs</u>. To this end, three underlying principles have been outlined, and the way in which the ATTENDING system implements each of these principles has been described. The relationship between each underlying principle and its implementation in ATTENDING is illustrated below:

PRINCIPLES	IMPLEMENTATION
1. Rough Criteria Eliminate Obviously Poor Choices	rough estimates of the "magnitude" of a risk
2. Domain-Specific Knowledge Focuses Attention on the Most Clinically Appropritate Alternatives	contextual preference rules
3. Discussion of Relevant Risks and Benefits in a Pertinent, Natural Way	pragmatic features

It is important to recognize that there is a distinction between the three principles, per se, and their current implementation in the ATTENDING system. As the development of ATTENDING continues, the _implementation_ of the principles may well be refined and augmented. It is anticipated, however, that the underlying principles themselves will remain constant.

6 Prose generation

The previous two chapters have described how ATTENDING explores alternative management choices, and how it is able to compare the relative risks and benefits in a natural way. ATTENDING's final task is to communicate its conclusions to its user. In so doing, the ability to make its points clearly is of paramount necessity.

Any author knows how difficult it is to write polished prose. Many rewritings may be required before satisfactory copy is finally produced. It is doubly difficult to write a program that produces readable prose for a complex analysis, especially since one must anticipate a variety of factors that may alter exactly what is to be said.

This section describes PROSENET, an approach used by ATTENDING to facilitate the generation of complex prose analysis. PROSENET uses as its backbone the Augmented Transition Network (ATN) formalism previously discussed in Chapter 4, with the unusual feature that prose fragments may be stored along the arcs of the ATN. (Thus, the ATTENDING system uses ATNs in two different ways: to structure its anesthetic knowledge, and to facilitate the generation of prose.) This approach to prose generation has the particular benefit of allowing a clean separation between the organization of the content of an analysis, and its actual expression in English prose.

Although PROSENET is being developed in a medical domain, its approach has broader potential. Indeed, as more and more mini- and micro-computers in everyday life find that they have relatively complex, yet well-defined, communications they wish to share with man, it will become increasingly desirable to facilitate their doing so. PROSENET represents one approach to this problem.

6.1 PROSENET IN PERSPECTIVE
Before PROSENET is described in detail, this section describes two other approaches that could be taken to the generation of a prose analysis by a machine.

6.1.1 A more ad-hoc approach

Many systems which produce prose output use a fairly ad-hoc approach. Sentences and sentence fragments are stored in the machine as "canned text". The control of the generation of this "canned text" is embedded in procedural logic, often in an ad-hoc way.

This approach can work well if the system's discussion is straightforward and predictable. If complex analysis is attempted, however, and the system designer wants flexibility for the discussion to vary depending on the particulars of the content, then this approach can become quite unwieldy.

There are a number of drawbacks. 1) The programming of the discussion itself becomes more difficult. 2) Any major revision in the prose output may involve substantial reprogramming. 3) The logic that generates the prose expression may become hopelessly interwoven with the logic that determines and organizes the content of the material to be discussed.

6.1.2 Sophisticated natural language genertion

At the other extreme, natural language (English prose) generation can be approached at a sophisticated level (McDonald 1980, Appelt 1982, McKeown 1982, Swartout 1982). Canned text is eschewed. Starting from underlying semantic entities, phrases and clauses are built up piece by piece. These are modified as appropriate by adjectives, adverbs, and modifying phrases, all dictated by the semantics of the domain and by the pragmatics of the particular discussion.

This approach is ambitious and is a major research direction in its own right. It therefore may not be practical for a system designer whose focus is on clinical problem solving rather than natural language research.

PROSENET represents a middle ground between these two extremes: an approach that is clean, but not so ambitious as to be a major project in its own right. PROSENET therefore is an applied computational linguistics approach to facilitate the implementation of systems which can produce polished prose.

6.2 PROSENET: AN ATN WITH PROSE FRAGMENTS STORED ALONG ITS ARCS

As previously mentioned in Chapter 4, the formalism of an ATN has been widely used in natural language systems. PROSENET's use of the ATN is unusual, however, in that prose fragments are stored along the ATN's arcs. When the ATN is used and the arcs are traversed, these prose fragments are output to produce the discussion.

To illustrate PROSENET's use of the ATN, Figure 6.1 shows three ATN networks in schematic form: #MULT_RISK, #RISK_S, and #RISK_NP. These are simplified versions of networks used to generate descriptions of medical risks.

As with the decision networks described in Chapter 4, each PROSENET ATN consists of states connected by arcs. Starting at the initial state, paths are traced through the network, following arcs from one state to another, ending whenever a POP arc is traversed. Whenever a PUSH arc is traversed, however, before the path can be continued, the system must first "push" to a second specified network, and trace a path through that network before "popping" back to the original network and continuing the path there.

The process of tracing such a path results in prose output being generated. For instance, different paths through the network #RISK_NP can generate the following prose:

```
...AT LEAST THE THEORETICAL RISK OF_____...
...AT LEAST THE THEORETICAL RISK THAT THIS COULD CAUSE_____...
...THE POSSIBLE RISK OF_____...
...THE RISK OF_____...
```

The exact path taken in discussing a particular risk is determined by "action routines" which augment the arcs. Each action routine activates or inactivates its arc depending on the pragmatic features of the risk being discussed, so that appropriate prose is generated. (The blanks above are filled in by a function, DESC_RISK, with a description of the risk involved, e.g. "HYPOTENSION", "BRONCHOSPASM", etc. The use of functions to generate prose is discussed below.)

Figure 6.2 shows how the states and arcs of the #RISK_NP network are written in PROSENET (as LISP data structures). The first state of the network, #RISK_NP, is defined below.

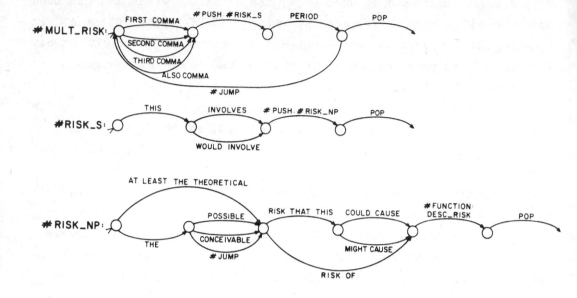

Figure 6.1 Three simplified PROSENET ATNs in schematic form.
(Miller 1983a, © 1983 IEEE)

```
(#RISK_NP ((AT LEAST THE THEORETICAL) #RNP20 THEOR_RISK)
          (THE #RNP10 T))

(#RNP10   (POSSIBLE #RNP20 POSS_RISK)
          (CONCEIVABLE #RNP20 CONC_RISK)
          (#JUMP #RNP20 T))

(#RNP20   ((#OPTION ((RISK OF) #RNP40 T)
                    ((RISK THAT THIS) #RNP30 T)) T T))

(#RNP30   ((#OPTION ((COULD CAUSE) #RNP40 T)
                    ((MIGHT CAUSE) #RNP40 T)) T T))

(#RNP40   ((#FUNCTION DESC_RISK) #RNP50 T))

(#RNP50   (#POP T T))
```

Figure 6.2 Internal representation of an example ATN.

```
(#RISK_NP ((AT LEAST THE THEORETICAL) #RNP20 THEOR_RISK)
          (THE #RNP10 T))
```

Two arcs leave this state. Each arc has three components: an ACTION, a
DESTINATION-STATE, and an ACTION ROUTINE. In the first arc, for instance,
the action is the prose fragment "AT LEAST THE THEORETICAL", the
destination state is #RNP20, and the action routine is named THEOR_RISK.

Eight different actions may be used in PROSENET. Three (PUSH, POP, and
JUMP) are conventional ATN primitives. The remaining five are unique to
PROSENET's use of the ATN, and are described below:

<u>A prose fragment</u> If a prose fragment is stored as the action of an arc,
then when that arc is traversed, the prose fragment is output in the
analysis being generated. This prose fragment may be either a single word,
a punctuation mark, or a parenthesized list of words and punctuation.

> example: ((FIRST COMMA) #NR5 IF_FIRST_RISK)

<u>A function call</u> If the action names a function, then that function is
called when the arc is traversed. Typically the function itself will then
generate prose. This gives the system designer the ability to embed some
of the prose generation in procedural logic if he so desires.

> example: ((#FUNCTION DESC_RISK) #RNP50 T)

<u>An OPTION arc</u> An OPTION arc specifies two or more alternative arcs, one of
which is chosen at random if the option arc itself is traversed.

> example: ((#OPTION (INVOLVES #GR20 T)
>   ((WOULD HAVE) #GR20 T)
>   ((MIGHT HAVE) #GR20 T)) T TEST_OPT)

Each time an OPTION arc is traversed, a different alternative is chosen
until all have been used, at which time it is reinitialized, never using
the same option twice in a row. OPTION arcs allow PROSENET to vary its
expression and avoid sounding monotonous.

<u>SEQUENCE and ENDSEQUENCE arcs</u> A SEQUENCE arc lists a number of alternative
arcs, which are to be chosen in sequence each time the SEQUENCE arc itself

is traversed.

```
example:   ((#SEQUENCE ((FIRST COMMA) #NS20 T)
                       ((SECOND COMMA) #NS20 T)
                       ((THIRD COMMA) #NS20 T)
                       ((FOURTH COMMA) #NS20 T)
                       ((ALSO COMMA) #NS20 T)) T TEST_SEQ)
```

If all arcs have been used, then the last arc is repeated. When an
ENDSEQUENCE arc is traversed, the list of arcs associated with the most
recently initiated SEQUENCE arc is reinitialized.

6.3 HOW PROSENET IS USED

As mentioned earlier, PROSENET allows the organization of the content of a
discussion to be separated cleanly from the generation of its prose
expression. To this end, ATTENDING first analyzes the anesthetist's plan
as described in Chapters 4 and 5, thereby determining the content of the
material to be discussed. The logic and the prose required to express this
content are all programmed into PROSENET ATNs. After the content has been
determined, the appropriate networks are activated to produce the prose
analysis.

In particular, for each major subpart of the anesthetic plan (induction,
intubation, maintenance), if there are major comments to be made, ATTENDING
places information describing the physician's chosen technique and any
suggested alternatives into global registers. It then activates the
particular PROSENET network which has been constructed to produce a
paragraph analyzing that aspect of the plan.

In a similar fashion, an introductory paragraph discussing management
principles, and later paragraphs discussing less major considerations are
produced.

In this way, ATTENDING organizes the overall order and the content of
the analysis by deciding the sequence of these various paragraphs, and by
placing into global registers the content of each paragraph's analysis.
The expression of this content is left entirely to PROSENET. From a
practical standpoint, this makes the generation of a prose analysis much
easier to implement and refine.

60

In fine-tuning the system's prose output, the system designer must anticipate every permutation of expression that may occur. This is difficult to do, and is bound to require iterative reworking and polishing before satisfactory output is consistently obtained. PROSENET simplifies this process since only the ATN networks need be massaged and modified in this fine-tuning process. The rest of the system need not be touched.

For instance, in an earlier version of ATTENDING, paragraph 2 of the first example critique in Chapter 3 read as follows:

INTUBATION OF THIS PATIENT IS CLEARLY IMPORTANT BECAUSE OF A FULL STOMACH. RAPID SEQUENCE INTUBATION IS A REASONABLE APPROACH. THE CHOICE OF SUCCINYLCHOLINE, HOWEVER, INVOLVES THE RISK OF INCREASED INTRAOCULAR PRESSURE, AND OF LIFE-THREATENING HYPERKALEMIA IF THE STROKE IS RECENT AND INVOLVES HEMIPARESIS. AN ALTERNATIVE WOULD BE HIGH DOSE PANCURONIUM. THIS WOULD HAVE THE RISK OF PROLONGED PARALYSIS DUE TO COMPROMISED RENAL EXCRETION. AN ALTERNATIVE APPROACH, PERHAPS, TO RAPID SEQUENCE INTUBATION WOULD BE INTUBATION AFTER MASK INDUCTION WITH CRICOID PRESSURE.

This discussion was changed to its present format solely by altering PROSENET ATNs. This took 1-2 hours of programming to accomplish. The rest of the ATTENDING system was not changed at all.

6.4 ENFORCING CONTEXTUAL CONSISTENCY IN PROSE EXPRESSION

An interesting distinction between content and expression which became apparent in implementing PROSENET concerns the need to make the different parts of the discussion mutually consistent. Many consistency constraints deal with the content of the analysis: ATTENDING should not advocate one overall approach in one part of the analysis, and a different approach elsewhere.

There are also, however, consistency contraints of a purely expressive nature. Without these expressive constraints, PROSENET may repeat itself in ways that are awkward and redundant. Although not strictly wrong, this often sounds unnatural. To prevent this redundancy, once a piece of information has been mentioned, any subsequent reference to it may have to be modified in some way to sound natural to the reader. (Pronominalization is one common instance of this phenomenon.)

Several of these constraints on expression are illustrated below. Some operate on the sentence level, others on the paragraph level, and still others globally at the level of the discussion as a whole.

6.4.1 A Sentence-Level Constraint

The following sentence illustrates an inadvertent redundancy that might occur within a single sentence:

...IN A PATIENT WITH HYPOVOLEMIA, THIS TECHNIQUE COULD HAVE RISK OF HYPOTENSION IN THE PRESENCE OF HYPOVOLEMIA.

Here, a medical problem (hypovolemia) is mentioned twice in a single sentence, once when introducing the discussion of a particular risk, and again when describing the risk itself. To avoid this duplication, arcs may be added to the appropriate ATN to delete the second (underlined) reference whenever it would be redundant, (i.e., if the sentence contains a prior reference to hypovolemia).

6.4.2 A Paragraph-Level Constraint

The following example demonstrates redundancy between different sentences in a paragraph:

...THE CHOICE OF MORPHINE, HOWEVER, COULD HAVE TWO POSSIBLE RISKS. FIRST, THERE IS THE RISK OF HYPOTENSION DUE TO HISTAMINE RELEASE. SECOND, IN THE PRESENCE OF ASTHMA, THERE IS THE RISK OF BRONCHOSPASM, AGAIN, TRIGGERED BY HISTAMINE RELEASE.

Here the same mechanism (histamine release) is involved in two risks being discussed. To sound most natural, the discussion of the second risk must be modified to acknowledge the prior reference. This can be done by inserting the underlined prose segment.

6.4.3 A Global Constraint

Redundant expression can also occur between different paragraphs.

IN REGARD TO INDUCTION, THE CHOICE OF HALOTHANE INVOLVES AT LEAST THE THEORETICAL RISK OF HALOTHANE INDUCED HEPATOTOXICITY. IT DOES, HOWEVER,

HAVE THE ADVANTAGE OF HELPING PREVENT BRONCHOSPASM SINCE HALOTHANE IS A BRONCHODILATOR. AN ALTERNATIVE WOULD BE ENFLURANE. HERE, HOWEVER, THERE IS THE CONCEIVABLE RISK THAT THIS COULD CAUSE INITIAL BRONCHOSPASM DUE TO AIRWAY IRRITABILITY. ALSO, IN A PATIENT WITH CHRONIC RENAL FAILURE, THERE IS AT LEAST THE THEORETICAL RISK OF RENAL TOXICITY DUE TO METABOLIC RELEASE OF FLUORIDE ION.

FROM THE STANDPOINT OF MAINTENANCE, INHALATIONAL TECHNIQUE HAS THE ADVANTAGE OF PREVENTING BRONCHOSPASM BY KEEPING THE ANESTHETIC LEVEL DEEP. THE CHOICE OF HALOTHANE INVOLVES CERTAIN CONSIDERATIONS WHICH HAVE ALREADY BEEN DISCUSSED. ...

Here the same technique (the choice of the inhalational anesthetic HALOTHANE) is used in two subparts of the plan. PROSENET must avoid repeating the underlined sentences in paragraph 1 which critique this technique. This can be done by replacing them in paragraph 2 as illustrated.

PROSENET enforces these expressive constraints by having three lists, one initialized at the start of each sentence, one at the start of each paragraph, and one at the start of the discussion as a whole. As problems, mechanisms, and techniques are discussed, each is recorded (by action routines) in the appropriate list. In this way PROSENET can later recognize (also by action routines) if the same material comes up again, and can modify its expression appropriately.

Thus, these expressive constraints can be handled solely by modifying the PROSENET ATNs, completely separate from the organization of the content of the analysis.

6.5 SUMMARY OF PROSENET'S APPROACH
PROSENET has been developed as part of the ATTENDING system to facilitate the generation of a complex prose analysis by a machine. Although developed in a medical domain, PROSENET has potential application wherever a machine has a complex, but well-defined, analysis to share with its users.

7 Discussion

7.1 CURRENT SYSTEM LIMITATIONS

ATTENDING is a system undergoing continued development. The ultimate goal is to accommodate an arbitrary patient with any of a broad range of medical problems. The current database is limited, however, as described below:

Anesthetic techniques   ATTENDING's ADNs currently include the greater portion of basic anesthetic techniques. In particular, it includes approximately 30 elemental techniques, and 20 non-elemental techniques. These may be modestly expanded and refined in the future.

Anesthetic implications of underlying problems   ATTENDING presently has problem management frames describing the anesthetic implications of 25 medical problems. This represents the main present database limitation. Knowledge of approximately 100-200 problems would probably be required for reasonably general use.

   Despite the currently limited database, however, the system is able to function as a consultant for a limited patient population. Also, its tutorial mode allows anesthetist self-evaluation using challenging cases, as illustrated in Chapter 3 and in Appendix I. Indeed, the 25 problems currently known to ATTENDING include a good number of the most interesting problems faced in anesthesia. As a result, numerous cases involving interesting risk tradeoffs can currently be discussed in the system's tutorial mode.

   The database constraint is not the only present limitation. ATTENDING focuses its advice around a central but circumscribed set of considerations in the preoperative formulation of an anesthetic plan. It does not, however, discuss the management of intraoperative problems at all. Furthermore, there are many preoperative management issues which ATTENDING does not presently address. Among these are:

(a) proposed invasive monitoring,

(b) fluid and electrolyte plans,

(c) preoperative considerations in preparing the patient medically for surgery,

(d) preoperative management of chronic medications.

It would certainly be interesting to expand the system to include certain of these issues.

The current work on ATTENDING, however, has focused on developing the approach of critiquing a physician's plan, concentrating on a very central set of considerations in anesthetic management. These happen to be particularly amenable to the type of risk-tradeoff analysis which the system is designed to perform. As a result, they provide a fertile environment for exploring the design issues outlined in the previous chapters.

7.2 THE RELATIONSHIP OF CRITIQUING AND RISK ANALYSIS

This section discusses how the critiquing approach allows ATTENDING to avoid dealing with certain issues of risk assessment in detail, and how in some respects this can be perceived as an advantage of the approach. As discussed in Chapter 5, the assessment of risk is central to critiquing. In this regard, it is interesting that critiquing places additional demands on the system designer, while at the same time allowing him to avoid certain difficult problems.

7.2.1 A critiquing system must deal explicitly with risk

In building a system to advocate a single approach to a patient's management, a system designer might well incorporate heuristics to prune the system's search tree, and thereby focus on certain approaches in the presence of certain disease states. These heuristics would reflect the designer's appreciation of the various risk tradeoffs involved. The system's knowledge of the risk tradeoffs, however, might be buried in these heuristics in an ad-hoc fashion. The system itself would therefore not be able to access and manipulate this knowledge in a general way.

To critique a physician's plan of management, ATTENDING must have its knowledge more flexibly organized than would be required if it merely formulated a single approach to the patient's management. The system designer must think through all the possible risks explicitly and systematically. He must then incorporate a comprehensive appreciation of risk tradeoffs into the system on several levels. In particular, the system must <u>know</u> about each risk, it must have a general mechanism for <u>comparing</u> risks, and it must be able to <u>discuss</u> risk tradeoffs articulately.

Thus, to critique a plan, ATTENDING must confront explicitly the underlying risk tradeoffs in a more complete way than is necessary in a system which formulates a single management approach. Without this extra knowledge, the system would not be able to react to an arbitrary plan. Thus, critiquing places certain extra demands on a system designer.

7.2.2 <u>A critiquing system need not assess each risk in detail</u>

At the same time, however, the critiquing approach relieves the system of certain difficulties involved in "fine-tuning" the anesthetist's approach to risk tradeoffs. For instance, in deciding how best to induce anesthesia for a patient with coronary artery disease (CAD) and a full stomach, a physician must first assess the severity of the CAD. This involves asking a broad set of questions: has the patient had a prior myocardial infarction (heart attack) and if so, how many and how recently; does he have angina and if so, how often and when; what is his excercise tolerance, etc. Once these questions are answered, the "best" approach still rests on the subjective judgement of the physician.

It would be frustrating to try to incorporate all these questions into the machine for every risk. It would also probably be fruitless, since different physicians frequently approach a patient differently given the same answers to the questions. Yet to fully evaluate any risk tradeoff, one must explore each risk in this fashion.

By taking the approach of critiquing a physician's plan, ATTENDING is able to avoid extremely detailed evaluation of each risk. It must have a flexible, general knowledge of the risks, and must be able to manipulate, evaluate, and discuss risks tradeoffs in general terms. The final weighing of the risks against one another, however, is left to the physician.

It would certainly be interesting to <u>augment</u> ATTENDING to assist the physician, if requested, in the detailed assessment of each risk. Such assistance is not currently attempted. In a non-critiquing system, such detailed assessment of individual risks would be necessary to allow it to advocate a "best" approach. Unfortunately, since this assessment can be quite subjective, it would be difficult if not impossible to incorporate into the computer. The interesting feature of critiquing is that it <u>allows</u> ATTENDING to defer this detailed evaluation of risk to the physician.

7.2.3 Summary: critiquing and risk
In summary, critiquing interplays with risk in two ways.

(a) Critiquing forces the system designer to confront explicitly the underlying risk tradeoffs involved in anesthetic management, and to incorporate these <u>in general terms</u> at several levels into the machine's analysis.

(b) At the same time, the system avoids the subjective fine-tuning required to fully assess each risk. Realistically, this can only be done by the physician who takes the ultimate responsibility for the patient's care.

8 Teaching with ATTENDING

As described in the previous chapters, ATTENDING is being developed with the goal of consultation regarding real patients. This consultation use, however, is currently limited since the patient must have some combination of the 25 medical problems known to the system. Nevertheless ATTENDING can be used for teaching using hypothetical cases. The 25 problems afford a variety of challenging cases with interesting risk tradeoffs. Section 8.1 describes how ATTENDING has been adapted experimentally to make this teaching as structured and enjoyable as possible.

In addition to its educational value, the tutorial use of ATTENDING is helping to test and "debug" the system's knowledge. There are a number of practical problems involved in the development of an expert system's knowledge base. Among these is the large amount of knowledge that may be required. The problem of testing this knowledge for accuracy, completeness, and consistency can be a formidible task. Section 8.2 describes how <u>tutorial use</u> of ATTENDING is helping to address these problems while the system's knowledge base is still in its formative stages.

8.1 <u>ADAPTING ATTENDING FOR TEACHING</u>

One might imagine using ATTENDING in a very straightforward way for teaching:

(a) ATTENDING describes a hypothetical case,
(b) a resident outlines a management plan,
(c) ATTENDING critiques the plan.

This straightforward use of the system, however, is somewhat stark and abrupt for teaching. The format is repetitive and lacks a global structure to tie the teaching session together. To help give structure and variety to ATTENDING's teaching activity, a teaching interface has been developed as illustrated in Figure 8.1. This teaching interface, which does not involve any modification of ATTENDING itself, has two main features:

<u>Different modes</u> It invokes ATTENDING in three different modes, thereby making the teaching session more varied, and allowing different types of issues to be explored.

<u>A clinical theme</u> It organizes the teaching session into an interactive "mini case conference" centered around a clinical theme, thereby giving structure to the session.

The two following subsections describe both of these teaching enchancements in turn.

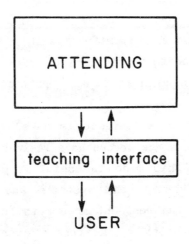

Figure 8.1 ATTENDING's teaching interface.

8.1.1 ATTENDING's three teaching modes

ATTENDING can be used for teaching in three modes. Each mode has certain advantages and allows certain types of management issues to be explored. In all three modes, a short paragraph describing a patient is first presented by ATTENDING, as illustrated in Chapter 3 and in the Appendix.

"BEST PLAN" mode Here an anesthesia resident is asked to propose a reasonable plan for ATTENDING to critique. This mode can help explore interesting management issues in both common and uncommon diseases. If, however, a standard anesthetic approach is satisfactory (such as thiopental, succinylcholine, ethrane, nitrous), certain interesting management issues may frequently not be confronted in this mode.

"CRITIQUE" mode Here ATTENDING presents the resident with a proposed plan containing management errors. The resident is asked to critique that plan himself, and then compare his critique with ATTENDING's. This mode can help explore the anesthetic implictions of less commonly used techniques, as well as specific management features of particular diseases.

"WORST PLAN" mode Here the resident is asked to propose a deliberately poor plan. He then lists the errors he perceives and compares this list to ATTENDING's analysis. This mode is useful from two standpoints: 1) It serves to test and "debug" the system's knowledge in a very direct fashion. 2) It allows the resident free rein in exercising his knowledge of the risks and benefits of different approaches to the patient's management.

Using these three modes, interesting anesthetic management issues can be explored in an interactive fashion. A resident can gain experience in formulating his anesthetic approach to complicated patients, and at the same time receive feedback to help him evaluate his approach.

8.1.2 Interactive "mini case conferences"

In experimenting with ATTENDING as a teaching tool, we have found it useful to create teaching modules, each structured around a clinical theme. These provide an organized structure for the teaching sessions. The Appendix, for

70

instance, shows a teaching session structured around the theme of "emergency inductions".

In this session, the computer introduces the theme with a brief discussion of the emergency induction of anesthesia. Next, three patients are described, and the resident is asked to propose a plan for each (in either BEST PLAN or WORST PLAN mode) or to critique a plan outlined by the computer (CRITIQUE mode). Finally, the computer types out a few related questions for the resident to think about. In this way, the session has the format of a "mini case conference" in which the management implications of several interesting patients are explored.

8.1.3 Summary: the two teaching enhancements

These two enhancements are computationally simple and do not involve any modification of the ATTENDING system itself. Nevertheless they do serve to make the sessions more structured and enjoyable.

As mentioned previously, the same system is used both for teaching and for consultation. The only internal difference is that for teaching, the patient's problems are already entered into the system, whereas for consultation, these problems are entered by the user. In the GUIDON/NEOMYCIN project (Clancey and Letsinger 1981; London and Clancey 1982), in contrast, a second expert system specifically designed for teaching was interfaced to MYCIN's diagnostic knowledge base to achieve a sophisticated teaching capability.

ATTENDING's goal, however, is not to explore issues of sophisticated computer-aided instruction, but rather to package the ATTENDING system so that it can be used experimentally for a practical purpose. This allows practical feedback from real users concerning ATTENDING's design and the critiquing approach in general.

We anticipate that the critiquing approach can be productively extended to many other areas of medical management. Experimental use of ATTENDING for teaching can provide practical experience with the approach, and thereby give insight as to domains where the approach might most profitably be applied, and as to the type of advice such a system might most usefully provide.

8.2 TEACHING AS A MODE OF EXPERT SYSTEM VALIDATION/EVALUATION

A major problem in the implementation of expert systems is assuring the quality of the systems' knowledge base. This knowledge must be complete, consistent, and accurate. One approach to quality assurance is to perform a formal validation, or evaluation, of the system's performance. On a less formal level, perhaps as a prelude to such validation, is the need to thoroughly test and "debug" the knowledge. One of the best ways to assure the reliability of a knowledge base is to use it extensively for a practical purpose.

Using a system for _teaching_ is a very effective way to use and reuse its knowledge, and thereby flush out any problems. It is a caveat of information processing that data which is stored but little used tends to be much less reliable than data which is used extensively. In this regard, tutorial use of a developmental knowledge base can serve a very productive purpose.

8.2.1 Incremental debugging of knowledge: management vs. diagnosis

Furthermore, as knowledge of additional medical problems is added, cases involving these problems can be included in those used for teaching. This allows incremental testing and debugging of the new knowledge as it is added.

It is important to point out that <u>a system like ATTENDING which critiques management has an advantage over diagnostic systems with respect to such incremental testing of knowledge</u>. In management, any underlying problem which a patient does <u>not</u> have, does <u>not</u> affect his management in any way. Knowledge of that problem could be removed from the knowledge base without affecting the analysis. As a result, when knowledge of a new problem is added, it will not affect the system's performance on existing cases not involving that problem. In contrast, in a diagnostic system, as knowledge of new diseases is added, they immediately become candidates for <u>every</u> patient's diagnosis. Therefore, previous <u>diagnostic</u> test cases which were working well may cease to do so as the knowledge base expands.

8.3 TEACHING: A DEVELOPMENTAL MILESTONE FOR CONSULTATION SYSTEMS

Most of the medical expert systems discussed in Chapter 2 have the ultimate goal of consultation for real patients. At present, however, almost all are still developmental. There are a number of reasons for this. First, many of the projects have tackled extremely ambitious domains. Also, many are attempting to incorporate sophisticated capabilities, such as explanation. Beyond these problems, however, there are obvious practical difficulties integrating computer advice into life-and-death decisions regarding real patients.

As a result, many medical expert system projects may find that applications involving hypothetical patients, such as teaching, are useful developmental milestones, with several potential advantages:

(a) The teaching activity may be valuable in its own right.

(b) The hypothetical patients used for teaching can be chosen in areas where the system's knowledge is known to be strong.

(c) The teaching activity can serve to give the system's knowledge extensive use, as discussed above.

(d) The teaching can also give the system builders practical feedback as to their system design.

For a number of reasons therefore, tutorial use of an expert medical system may be a valuable milestone along the way to eventual consultation use. ATTENDING's current teaching activity demonstrates one way in which this milestone can be achieved.

9 Current status and future directions

The previous chapters have described the ATTENDING system and its critiquing approach to computer advice, together with the rationale for critiquing from both a clinical and an AI standpoint. This final chapter summarizes the various results that have been obtained to date. It discusses several ways in which the critiquing approach might be extended, including some projects already in progress. It also discusses a number of ways in which the ATTENDING system itself might be extended and made more sophisticated.

9.1 SUMMARY OF RESULTS

The implementation of ATTENDING has touched on a number of fields: clinical decision-making, decision modelling, expert system design, risk analysis, and natural language generation. This section summarizes the ATTENDING project's contributions in these areas.

9.1.1 Critiquing

The critiquing approach is the primary focus of the ATTENDING project. Critiquing represents a different approach to computer-based advice. Critiquing may prove well suited for medicine, for other domains where decisions are quite subjective, and perhaps even for certain domains where objective decision criteria exist.

From the standpoint of computer science, critiquing can be perceived as a mode of _explanation_ which lets a system structure its advice around the particular concerns of the user in a direct and natural way. As such, it contributes to the field of expert system design a new modality for using an expert knowledge base. Critiquing can be seen as a particular control strategy for accessing knowledge and presenting it to the user.

From the standpoint of medical practice, critiquing has a number of potential social, medical, and medicolegal advantages which were outlined in Chapter 1. In particular, critiquing allows the physician to be the final decision-maker. The computer is never forced to commit itself to one approach or another. In the face of the tremendous subjectivity and variation in medical practice, a computer advisor which does not take the critiquing approach, but rather tries to tell a physician what to do, may be undertaking an extremely difficult, and ultimately self-defeating task.

9.1.2 The ATN: a hierarchical model for decision analysis

ATTENDING uses the Augmented Transition Network formalism to structure its knowledge of alternative anesthetic choices. The ATN offers a hierarchical structure in which the decisions of anesthetic management fit very naturally.

When compared to clinical decision analysis (Weinstein 1980), the ATN has several advantages over the widely used decision-tree. As was discussed in Chapter 4, the ATN allows 1) a hierarchical structure, and 2) certain representational efficiencies since paths which diverge can later rejoin.

When compared to certain planning formalisms developed in Artificial Intelligence research (Sacerdoti 1977; Stefik 1981), ATTENDING's use of the ATN is somewhat limited since it does not address a number of sophisticated issues. There is no formal mechanism, for instance, for handling interactions between subplans. As discussed in Chapter 4, this was not needed in the anesthestic domain.

The ATN formalism, originally developed for language processing, has been used as a model of decision making (M Miller and Goldstein 1977). It has not, however, been used previously in medical expert systems. ATTENDING's use of the ATN helps to highlight the hierarchical nature of many medical decisions and to point up the need for a decision model which captures this hierarchical character.

9.1.3 Risk analysis as the process underlying medical management

A further contribution of the ATTENDING project has been to focus on risk analysis as the underlying process of medical management. Although most physicians may not consciously think in terms of risk analysis when managing patients, the centrality of risk is nevertheless clear.

A system that does not critique, but rather tries to advocate optimal management, is not forced to confront risk explicitly. In such a system, knowledge of risk may well be buried implicitly in the heuristics that determine optimal management. In other words, the system's knowledge of risk may be "compiled" into the decision-making rules. The system designers may not even recognize that this has occurred.

In contrast, a critiquing system must not only be able to propose a good plan, it must also be able to react to any approach (good, marginal, or poor). To do this, it must be able to analyze the relative merits of alternatives, and explicitly discuss the relevant risks and benefits involved.

Such manipulation and explicit discussion of risk cannot be readily performed if the system's knowledge of risk is "compiled" into decision heuristics. The knowledge must be explicitly available so that it can be accessed "interpretively": so that it can be inspected and manipulated. The designer of a critiquing system is therefore forced to deal in a very explicit and comprehensive way with the risks and risk tradeoffs. As a result, critiquing serves to highlight risk as a central issue in medical management.

9.1.4 A heuristic approach to risk analysis

Aside from ATTENDING's overall focus on risk analysis as the underlying process of medical management, the system also implements a particular approach to risk, the heuristic approach described in Chapter 5.

The application of heuristic techniques to risk analysis in a formal fashion differs from conventional approaches to risk. Formal risk analysis has been largely statistical. It is clear, however, that for many real-world domains statistics may be either 1) not available, 2) too massive to compile, or 2) impractical to obtain. For instance, the only way to obtain certain statistics regarding anesthetic management would be to manage selected groups of patients poorly and document the complications that occurred: a clearly impractical project.

Medicine is a very rich domain for exploring issues of risk. The development of a robust, heuristic approach to risk, however, could have potential application in many areas outside of medicine. The current ATTENDING implementation is a first step in this direction.

9.1.5 Polished prose generation by an expert system

Current expert systems tend to use canned text for communication with their users. Some use text fragments associated with inference rules to help generate rule-based explanation. At the same time, a subfield of AI is working on the sophisticated generation of natural language, and on the very interesting and difficult linguistic issues involved.

ATTENDING has set itself an intermediate goal: developing a flexible formalism to facilitate the generation of polished prose. Although the PROSENET approach is clearly closer in spirit to canned text generation than to sophisticated language generation, it does allow the system designer great flexibility to manipulate, massage, and refine the system's prose output, independent of the rest of the system's analysis.

Thus PROSENET contributes to the field of expert system design: 1) a specific design goal (polished prose) for an expert system's output, and 2) a formalism, implemented in ATTENDING, which can help to acheive that goal.

9.1.6 Teaching as a mode of expert system validation/evaluation

Validation and evaluation of an expert system is a major problem especially in view of the large amounts of knowledge that may be involved. Some testing can be done in the laboratory. Certainly there are various tests a system itself may make for internal consistency (Suwa et al. 1982), and there are tools which may assist a designer in evaluating the system's knowledge. (Politakis and Weiss 1981)

Nevertheless there is no substitute for subjecting the knowledge, and the system as a whole, to a practical use. There are obvious drawbacks, however, to practical consultation use of a system as a method of debugging its knowledge base.

Tutorial use of ATTENDING while still under development allows the knowledge to be exercised, and the system itself to be tested, by real users for a practical purpose. As discussed in Chapter 8, this can be done incrementally as knowledge is added to the system. Since hypothetical cases are used, any errors or inconsistencies will not affect the care of real patients. Indeed, it may be tutorially useful (as demonstrated in ATTENDING's "WORST PLAN" mode) to ask the user to make deliberate errors and see if the system reacts appropriately. In this way, the system's knowledge can be debugged in a very direct fashion by tutorial use.

Beyond the issues outlined above, it is our hope that the critiquing approach implemented in ATTENDING may serve as a model for similar systems in other areas of medicine, and outside of medicine. To this end, the next section discusses possible extensions of the approach.

9.2 EXTENDING THE CRITIQUING APPROACH

A major current goal of the ATTENDING project is to extend critiquing into other areas of medicine. We anticipate that the approach will have wide application.

It may turn out, however, that certain areas are better suited for critiquing than others. For instance, if there is only a single approach to a problem, then critiquing will not be very helpful unless the approach is so complicated that a physician has difficulty remembering it. Similarly, if there are several approaches and the physician is free to use any one with no particular risks or benefits, then here again critiquing will have little to contribute.

Characteristics which may make an area of medicine suitable for the critiquing approach are:

When many alternatives exist A number of areas in medicine have experienced a proliferation of management alternatives. Two examples are 1) the pharmacologic management of essential hypertension, and 2) antibiotic therapy. In such areas, a critiquing computer system could help the physician sort through the various alternatives and give him feeback as to their relative pros and cons.

When the alternatives are changing rapidly In a number of areas, not only are there many alternatives, but the alternatives are changing rapidly as new drugs, new tests, and new techniques are developed. A critiquing system could help a physician keep abreast of this new knowledge, in the context of daily patient care.

When many risks and benefits exist in different patients Typically the reason that many alternatives are developed is that none is ideal. Different choices have relative advantages and disadvantages in different patients. A discussion of these indications and contraindications fits

78

naturally into critiquing advice.

Thus there are a number of characteristics which may make a domain suitable for the critiquing approach. The following subsections discuss three general areas of medicine where such domains might be found: 1) medical management, 2) medical work-up, and 3) diagnosis.

9.2.1 Critiquing medical management
There are currently several developmental systems which extend the critiquing approach beyond anesthesia into other areas of medical management.

9.2.1.1 HT-ATTENDING (essential hypertension)
HT-ATTENDING has been developed to critique the pharmacologic management of essential hypertension (Miller and Black 1984). Essential hypertension is an excellent domain for exploring critiquing for several reasons:

It is frequently encountered by the physician Not only is hypertension widely encountered by the general practitioner, it is familiar to almost every physician. In contrast, anesthetic management is relatively esoteric, and most doctors are not familiar with the issues involved. As a result, the domain of hypertension is more visible to the medical community as a whole. In addition, hypertension itself is currently receiving a great deal of attention as a major health problem. This heightened visibility of hypertension as a domain may enhance the visibility of the critiquing approach, and perhaps allow the system to serve as a model for similar systems in other areas of primary medical care.

There is a bewildering array of treatment alternatives A physician treating essential hypertension is faced with many treatment modalities (diuretics, beta blockers, central alpha agonists, alpha blockers, vasodilators, channel blockers, converting enzyme inhibitors) with several different drugs within each category. New drugs are constantly coming on the market (five in the past year).

<u>A host of risks and benefits exist</u> Each drug has specific risks and benefits in different patients. Studies are frequently published evaluating the relative efficacy of different drugs and different combinations in certain patients. It is virtually impossible for the practicing physician to keep abreast of all this information.

The following excerpt illustrates HT-ATTENDING's operation. Here, a hypertensive patient who also happens to have gout is being started on antihypertensive treatment. A physician has suggested hydrochlorothiazide 50 mg bid, a not uncommon initial regimen. In the following excerpt, HT-ATTENDING discusses the plan at several levels including dosage, mentioning alternatives, and documenting one recommendation with a reference (Materson et al. 1978).

"In the United States, diuretics are recommended by most authorities as initial or step one therapy. Since the initiation of diuretic therapy may precipitate a gouty attack, you may wish to start prophylactic treatment when beginning a diuretic in a patient with gout.

"A thiazide diuretic or similar acting agent is the drug of choice for most patients. Hydrochlorothiazide is a commonly used thiazide diuretic. Chlorthalidone or metolazone are alternative agents worth considering since they are long-acting and can be given once a day. We usually start treatment with a lower dose than the dose you propose. We now recommend treatment with hydrochlorothiazide 25 mg qd or bid. Recent work by Materson (1) has shown that low doses or diuretics may be as effective as higher doses yet cause less hypokalemia."

In managing hypertension, a physician starts with one drug and periodically either increases dosage or adds further agents, until blood pressure is finally (hopefully) controlled. HT-ATTENDING is able to help at each step of this process. HT-ATTENDING is designed to give a physician feedback as to how his approach to a particular patient fits in with current thinking in the field and the current spectrum of agents available. HT-ATTENDING is still undergoing evaluation and refinement.

9.2.1.2 VQ-ATTENDING (ventilator management)

VQ-ATTENDING is a system under development to critique aspects of the ventilatory management of a patient receiving mechanical respiratory support. In the excerpt below, for a patient whose arterial oxygenation is good, a physician has suggested a change in ventilator settings: decreasing the inspired oxygen (FiO2) while leaving airway pressure (PEEP) unchanged. The current developmental system responds as follows:

"In regard to oxygenation, there are several goals for this patient's management. One goal is to maintain an adequate paO2. A second goal is to reduce the risks associated with high PEEP. A third goal is to reduce the level of oxygenation support.

"You have suggested a moderate decrease in FiO2, to 0.4. Once an adequate oxygenation can be obtained with an FiO2 of .6, we normally concentrate on lowering PEEP if it is high. We therefore would suggest an FiO2 of .6 for the time being. You have proposed leaving PEEP at 12. A decrease in PEEP is probably possible."

Ventilator management differs from anesthesia and hypertension in a number of ways. Several management decisions involve choosing from a continuum of alternatives. For instance, inspired oxygen can range from 20% to 100%, and airway pressure (PEEP) can vary from 0 to a practical maximum of 30-40 cm H2O, etc. Finding appropriate settings for a particular patient often involves a process of adjustment and readjustment over a period of time. There is no rigorously correct way to do this, and individual physicians do it somewhat differently. In the face of this variation, the critiquing approach may prove particularly useful.

9.2.1.3 ONCOCIN (oncology protocols)

In addition to the systems described above, the ONCOCIN system (Shortliffe et al. 1981) developed at Stanford has also recently been adapted experimentally to a critiquing mode of advice (Langlotz and Shortliffe 1983). ONCOCIN's domain, oncology management, is unusual in medicine in that established protocols dictate how oncologic agents are given. As a result, whereas the ATTENDING systems may discuss the pros and cons of several alternative approaches, ONCOCIN is able to critique by indicating how the proposed management differs from its <u>objective</u> criteria (the protocol). Thus ONCOCIN illustrates that the critiquing approach may also be useful when objective criteria exist.

In summary, critiquing has been experimentally introduced into several areas of medical management beyond anesthesiology and shows promise as a modality for advice in these domains.

9.2.2 Critiquing Medical Work-up

Work-up is an important area of medicine which lies between diagnosis and management. In work-up, a physician starts with a differential diagnosis, and proceeds to order tests to rule-in or rule-out a particular problem, or to assess its character and severity. Examples are 1) ordering x-ray and endoscopic procedures to evaluate GI bleeding, 2) ordering laboratory tests to rule out hyper- or hypo-thyroidism, or 3) investigating possible underlying causes of high blood pressure.

As in management, there may be a variety of different tests and procedures available in working up a given problem. New tests and procedures are periodically developed which may have advantages over previous tests, either overall or in certain patients. A critiquing system could tell the physician when his planned work-up involved tests or procedures which might be redundant, inappropriate, or incorrectly sequenced. Here again, the system could indicate alternative approaches and discuss the relative advantages of each.

There are usually several ways to approach the work-up of a given problem. Merely listing one approach is of no major help to the physician. Also, the mere listing of a sequence of tests and procedures is computationally trivial. This may be why work-up has not received much independent attention as an area for sophisticated computer advice. Once one takes a critiquing approach to work-up, however, the system design problems become much more interesting. Work-up may prove to be a very fruitful area for the critiquing approach.

9.2.3 Critiquing diagnosis

Most diagnostic programs have attempted to undertake the entire process of diagnosis: gathering information, processing it, and producing a differential diagnosis to guide further work-up. Some of the difficulties of this approach to computer-assisted diagnosis are discussed in Chapter 2.

An alternative approach would be a critiquing system to _help_ a physician confirm or refute his own diagnosis. Here a physician would describe a patient and indicate the (differential) diagnosis he had developed. In his description, he could mention any pertinent positive or negative findings which helped to confirm his diagnosis or which helped to rule out others.

The critiquing system could then mention further findings or tests the physician might like to check. It could also discuss the adequacy with which he had confirmed his diagnosis and ruled out other possibilities. In this way, a critiquing system could be a _diagnostic aid_ to help the physician refine his own diagnosis, rather than trying to perform the entire task for him.

Such a diagnostic aid might fit more naturally into the clinical environment. In fact, daily at "morning report", interns and residents across the country present their hospital admissions to senior staff, who critique their findings and conclusions in the fashion described above.

9.3 EXPANDING THE SCOPE OF ATTENDING'S ADVICE

The current implementation of ATTENDING is limited in a number of significant ways, some of which were discussed in Chapter 8. These limitations include:

Limitations in scope Although ATTENDING addresses certain central phases of anesthetic management, many important aspects of perioperative patient management are not considered.

Gaps of knowledge The system's knowledge of anesthetic alternatives is moderately restricted. Its knowledge of anesthetic implications of underlying medical problems is significantly limited.

Shallowness of knowledge The system's current knowledge of anesthetic risks and benefits is shallow. The system can compare and manipulate these risks internally and discuss them with the user, but only in very general terms.

These limitations still allow the system to be used experimentally for teaching, but even this teaching use of ATTENDING has limitations. As presently constructed, ATTENDING is probably best used for teaching relatively inexperienced anesthetists-in-training (nurse anesthetists or anesthesiology residents) rather than experienced pratitioners. For the more experienced anesthetist, one should probably include more detailed, specific information about the various risks and risk tradeoffs. This might include discussion of:

(a) the mechanisms of certain risks,
(b) specific studies evaluating different approaches to particular risk tradeoffs,
(c) the rationale for using more esoteric, less common approaches in certain patients,
(d) the different management philosophies of different institutions.

Each of these enhancements could certainly be added to ATTENDING. Each might in fact be added in either a quite straightforward way, or in a more complex and sophisticated way.

Our philosophy to date in developing ATTENDING, however, has been to restrict the system to a manageable set of problems. The emphasis has been to focus on the critiquing process itself, explore its basic nature, and get practical experience using it in a teaching tool. As this experience accumulates, we will gain more insights as to which enhancements might be most productive, and how best to incorporate them into critiquing advice.

9.4 A FINAL WORD

Most medical computer-advisors embody a single approach to a problem. As a result, to use the system, a physician must adapt himself to this built-in approach. On the other hand, there are often several ways to approach a medical problem, none clearly superior. There may also be ways which, although suboptimal, are adequate for the task. As a result, one would prefer a computer system to adapt itself and its advice to the approach of

84

the physician, rather than the other way around.

In this regard, a rough analogy might be made to the difference between a program that runs interpretively and one that is compiled. In directing a patient's management, a doctor behaves "interpretively". He looks at the patient's problems and their inherent risks, and at his available treatment options each with its risk and benefits. Finally, balancing these various risks and benefits against one another, he chooses his next step. He does this incrementally as he goes along, "interpretively" feeling his way through a maze of possibilities.

A computer program which attempts to preselect a method of traversing this maze of possibilities, in effect, "pre-compiles" the options into a single inflexible approach, ignoring the room for variation. Much more desirable is a computer system which leaves the options intact, is able to help assess the inherent risks and benefits, and allows the physician to use his judgment and experience to guide it "interpretively", through the many possible choices. At each step, the computer could help formulate and analyze the various options, but leave the ultimate decision to the physician. The current implementation of ATTENDING is a first step in exploring how to incorporate this type of flexibility into a machine.

Appendix I An example teaching session

Appendix I illustrates the teaching use of ATTENDING, and also gives further examples of the system's critiques. In particular, it shows a teaching session whose theme is the emergency induction of anesthesia. In the computer output that follows, all input typed by the user is underlined. Any comments inserted for the reader are enclosed in parentheses.

(The teaching module introduces itself with a brief stored overview of the session theme.)

EMERGENCY INDUCTIONS

Induction of anesthesia for emergency surgery can be fraught with many risks depending on the acute situation and on the patient's underlying medical problems. In planning an induction for an emergency case, two considerations are particularly important:

1. the possibility of a full stomach,
2. the patient's volume status.

The interaction of these two central considerations with a patient's other problems can lead to a host of potential risks and risk trade-offs. At times the optimal anesthetic approach to one problem may also be beneficial for another, but often it is not.

* *

case 1: Here a particular agent can be beneficial for two problems.

For the following case, select a reasonable management plan.

(Next the first hypothetical teaching case is presented. The user is asked to select a reasonable plan, the BEST PLAN mode. In the user's replies, however, we have included errors to help illustrate more fully aspects of the system's critique.)

- PATIENT HISTORY -

   A thirty four year old male with a history of asthma requiring several past hospitalizations comes to surgery after an auto accident for repair of a likely fractured spleen. His blood pressure is 85/50. He recently ate lunch.

- PLEASE OUTLINE A PLAN -

(The user outlines his plan by a process of menu selection.)

*** PREMED: 1-NONE 2-ATROPINE 3-GLYCOPYRROLATE 4-MORPHINE
   5-DEMEROL 6-FENTANYL 7-VALIUM 8-PENTOBARBITAL 9-SECONAL
   10-VISTARIL 11-DROPERIDOL 12-PHENERGAN
   type one or more numbers separated by spaces ***<u>2 4</u>

   type 1 if general ... 2 if regional ***<u>1</u>

*** INDUCTION: 1-THIOPENTAL 2-KETAMINE 3-HALOTHANE 4-ENFLURANE
   select one ***<u>1</u>

*** INTUBATION: 1-NONE 2-CONVENTIONAL 3-RAPIDSEQ 4-AWAKE_ORAL
   5-AWAKE_NASAL 6-MASKCRICOID 7-SUCCINYLCHOLINE 8-CURARE
   9-PANCURONIUM 10-FLAXEDIL 11-METUBINE
   type one or more numbers separated by spaces ***<u>3 7</u>

*** MAINTENANCE: 1-HALOTHANE 2-ENFLURANE 3-N2O 4-O2 5-MORPHINE
   6-DEMEROL 7-FENTANYL 8-CURARE 9-PANCURONIUM 10-FLAXEDIL
   11-METUBINE
   type one or more numbers separated by spaces ***<u>2 3 4</u>

```
*** you have selected:
    1 general
    2 premedication - ATROPINE MORPHINE
    3 induction - THIOPENTAL
    4 intubation - RAPIDSEQ SUCCINYLCHOLINE
    5 maintenance - ENFLURANE N2O O2
    type 0 if ok ... else number for change ***0
```

(Next ATTENDING produces its critique of this plan for this patient's management. As described in Chapter 6, these paragraphs are not stored text, but rather are pieced together from words and sentence fragments tailored to the particular plan and patient.)

There are a number of basic principles involved in this patient's management. First, in a patient with asthma, one must consider the problem of bronchospasm. Second, in the presence of hypovolemia, one must attempt to prevent hypotension. Third, a patient with a full stomach must be protected from aspiration.

Intubation of this patient is definitely appropriate because of a full stomach. Rapid sequence intubation is a reasonable approach. This, however, might have the conceivable risk of bronchospasm. An alternative approach to rapid sequence intubation would be intubation after mask induction with cricoid pressure.

In regard to induction, induction using thiopental would have two possible risks. First, there is the conceivable risk that this could cause bronchospasm. Second, in a patient with hypovolemia, there is the possible risk of hypotension. An alternative approach to induction using thiopental would be induction with ketamine. This has the advantage of helping to avoid hypotension since ketamine is supportive of blood pressure, and of suppressing bronchospasm since ketamine is a bronchodilator.

From the standpoint of maintenance, inhalational technique has the advantage of preventing bronchospasm by keeping the anesthetic level deep. On the other hand, it involves the risk of hypotension in the presence of hypovolemia. The choice of enflurane could have the conceivable risk of initial bronchospasm due to airway irritability. An alternative would be halothane. This has the advantage of helping prevent bronchospasm since halothane is a bronchodilator. An alternative approach to inhalational technique would be balanced anesthesia. This involves the risk of possible bronchospasm due to light anesthesia. It does, however, have the advantage of maintaining blood pressure.

Looking at other aspects of the proposed plan, there are two considerations worth mentioning.

1. Using no relaxant for maintenance might have the risk of inadequate surgical relaxation.

2. Morphine premedication would have the conceivable risk of bronchospasm due to histamine release.

* *

case 2: Heart disease and a full stomach is a classic combination.

For the following case, select a reasonable management plan.

- PATIENT HISTORY -
    A seventy five year old man with a history of three past heart attacks and subsequent angina comes to the operating room on an emergency basis with abdominal pain for repair of an abdominal aneurysm which is threatening to rupture. He recently ate.

- PLEASE OUTLINE A PLAN -

*** PREMED: 1-NONE 2-ATROPINE 3-GLYCOPYRROLATE 4-MORPHINE
    5-DEMEROL 6-FENTANYL 7-VALIUM 8-PENTOBARBITAL 9-SECONAL
    10-VISTARIL 11-DROPERIDOL 12-PHENERGAN
    type one or more numbers separated by spaces ***7

```
      type 1 if general ... 2 if regional ***1


*** INDUCTION:  1-THIOPENTAL  2-KETAMINE  3-HALOTHANE  4-ENFLURANE
    select one ***3


*** INTUBATION:  1-NONE  2-CONVENTIONAL  3-RAPIDSEQ  4-AWAKE_ORAL
    5-AWAKE_NASAL  6-MASKCRICOID  7-SUCCINYLCHOLINE  8-CURARE
    9-PANCURONIUM  10-FLAXEDIL  11-METUBINE
    type one or more numbers separated by spaces ***3 7


*** MAINTENANCE:  1-HALOTHANE  2-ENFLURANE  3-N2O  4-O2  5-MORPHINE
    6-DEMEROL  7-FENTANYL  8-CURARE  9-PANCURONIUM  10-FLAXEDIL
    11-METUBINE
    type one or more numbers separated by spaces ***7 9 3 4


*** you have selected:
    1 general
    2 premedication - VALIUM
    3 induction - HALOTHANE
    4 intubation - RAPIDSEQ SUCCINYLCHOLINE
    5 maintenance - FENTANYL PANCURONIUM N2O O2
    type 0 if ok ... else number for change ***0
```

There are a number of basic principles involved in this patient's management. First, in the presence of an abdominal aortic aneurysm, one must attempt to prevent aneurysmal rupture. Second, in a patient with coronary artery disease, one must consider the problem of hypotension and ischemia. Third, a patient with a full stomach must be protected from aspiration.

Intubation of this patient is clearly important because of a full stomach. Rapid sequence intubation may not be the best approach. This involves the conceivable risk of cardiac compromise. An alternative approach to rapid sequence intubation would be intubation after mask induction with cricoid pressure. This has the advantage of helping avoid hypotension. Intubation after mask induction with cricoid pressure may be preferable for a patient with coronary artery disease, if severe, since it allows more gradual induction with less danger of sudden cardiac decompensation.

In regard to induction, a gentle inhalational induction could have the risk of hypotension. An alternative approach, perhaps, to a gentle inhalational induction would be induction using thiopental. This might have the conceivable risk that this could cause hypotension from cardiac depression.

From the standpoint of maintenance, balanced anesthesia involves the conceivable risk of aneurysmal rupture induced by hypertension. An alternative approach to balanced anesthesia would be inhalational technique. This may be preferable for a patient with an abdominal aortic aneurysm since it allows more control of blood pressure and therefore less chance of aneurysmal rupture.

* *

case 3: Sometimes it's not the induction agent that causes the problems.

You are senior resident on call. Your madcap junior resident describes a patient, and his plan for anesthetic mangement. See how your critique compares to ATTENDING's.

(Here the system presents a case in the CRITIQUE mode. It happens to be the same case and management plan shown in Chapter 3. The wording of ATTENDING's critique, however, may be subtly altered. This is due to the use of OPTION arcs, which have the effect that successive generations of the same critique are not identical.)

- PATIENT HISTORY -
A sixty year old man, with a longstanding history of chronic renal failure and a prior stroke, comes to surgery for repair of a metal splinter embedded in his right eye. He recently ate lunch.

INDUCTION: THIOPENTAL
INTUBATION: RAPIDSEQ SUCCINYLCHOLINE
MAINTENANCE: HALOTHANE CURARE N20 02

Please jot down, or note mentally, any errors in this plan, plus any alternatives you might suggest.
type 'DONE' when you are finished.

DONE? --*DONE

There are a number of basic principles involved in this patient's management. First, in the presence of chronic renal failure, one must attempt to prevent renal toxicity and compromised renal excretion of drugs. Second, in a patient with a prior stroke, one must consider the problem of hyperkalemia. Third, a patient with a penetrating eye wound must be protected from eye morbidity. Fourth, in a patient with a full stomach, one must consider the problem of aspiration.

Intubation of this patient is certainly necessary because of a full stomach. Rapid sequence intubation is a reasonable approach. The choice of succinylcholine, however, would have two possible risks. First, there is the risk of eye morbidity from increased intraocular pressure. Second, if the stroke is recent and involves hemiparesis, there is the risk of life-threatening hyperkalemia. An alternative would be high dose pancuronium. Here, however, in a patient with chronic renal failure, there is the risk that this could cause prolonged postoperative paralysis due to compromised renal excretion. Thus there is no ideal way to perform rapid sequence intubation. An alternative approach, perhaps, to rapid sequence intubation would be intubation after mask induction with cricoid pressure.

Looking at other aspects of the proposed plan, for a patient with chronic renal failure, curare is a good choice since it is reliably metabolized by the liver, and halothane is appropriate since it has minimal nephrotoxicity.

92

* *

(At this point, the three hypothetical cases of the session are finished.
A few review questions relevant to emergency induction of anesthesia are
output, after which the user is free to quit, or to select another teaching
session.)

REVIEW QUESTIONS

1. ketamine -

   What does ketamine do to sympathetic tone?   how?
   What is its direct effect on the heart?
   What is its direct effect on the peripheral vasculature?
   In what patients is it likely to cause an increase in BP?
   In what patients is it likely to maintain BP?
   In what patients might it cause a precipitous collapse in BP?

2. thiopental -

   What direct effect does thiopental have on the heart?
   What direct effect on the peripheral vasculature?
   Can it release histamine?
   Can it affect sympathetic tone?

Appendix II The ATN of anesthetic management alternatives

Appendix II shows the Augmented Transition Network (ATN) currently used by ATTENDING to structure its knowledge of anesthetic management. The ATN is expressed as a LISP data structure and consists of a sequence of states. Each state is a list which starts with a state name (e.g. ANES, GA, REGIONAL) followed by a one or more arcs. Each arc is a list of three elements:

(a) the name of an anesthetic agent or technique,
(b) a destination state, and
(c) the name of the action routine associated with that arc.

```
(ANES (GA AN1 TGA)
      (REGIONAL AN1 TREG))
(AN1 (PREMED AN2 TPREM)
     (NOPREMED AN2 TNOPREMEDS))
(AN2 (POP T T))


(GA (INTUBATION G2 TINTUB))
(G2 (MAINTENANCE G3 TMAINT))
(G3 (INDUCTION G4 TINDUCT))
(G4 (POP T T))


(INTUBATION (AWAKE INT1 TAWAKE)
            (NONE INT1 TNOINTUB)
            (MASKCRICOID INT1 TMASKCRICOID)
            (RAPIDSEQ INT1 TRAPIDSEQ)
            (CONVENTIONAL INT1 TNORMINT))
(INT1 (POP T T))
```

```
(AWAKE (AWAKE_ORAL AW1 TORAL)
        (AWAKE_NASAL AW1 TNASAL))
(AW1 (POP T T))


(MASKCRICOID (RELAXANT MC1 TRELINT)
              (NORELAXANT MC1 TNOIRELAXANT))
(MC1 (POP T T))


(RAPIDSEQ (SUCCINYLCHOLINE RS1 TSUX)
           (PANCURONIUM RS1 THIGHPAV))
(RS1 (POP T T))


(CONVENTIONAL (RELAXANT NI1 TRELINT)
               (NORELAXANT NI1 TNOIRELAXANT))
(NI1 (POP T T))


(INDUCTION (INHAL IND1 TINHALIN)
            (THIOPENTAL IND1 TTPL)
            (KETAMINE IND1 TKETAMINE))
(IND1 (POP T T))


(MAINTENANCE (N20 M1 TN20)
              (NON20 M1 TNON20))
(M1 (RELAXANT M2 TRELAXANT)
     (NORELAXANT M2 TNORELAXANT))
(M2 (INHAL M3 TINHAL)
     (BALANCED M3 TBALANCED))
(M3 (POP T T))


(INHAL (HALOTHANE INH1 THALO)
        (ENFLURANE INH1 TETH))
(INH1 (POP T T))
```

```
(RELAXANT (SUCCINYLCHOLINE REL1 TSUX)
          (CURARE REL1 TDTC)
          (FLAXEDIL REL1 TGALL)
          (METUBINE REL1 TMET)
          (PANCURONIUM REL1 TPAV))
(REL1 (POP T T))


(BALANCED (MORPHINE B1 TMORPH)
          (DEMEROL B1 TDEM)
          (FENTANYL B1 TFENT))
(B1 (POP T T))


(PREMED (ANTICHOL PM1 TANTI)
        (NOANTICHOL PM1 TNOANTI))
(PM1 (SEDATIVE PM2 TSED)
     (NOSEDATIVE PM2 TNOSED))
(PM2 (POP T T))


(SEDATIVE (NARCOTIC SED2 TPMNARC)
          (NONARCOTIC SED2 TNONARCOTIC))


(NARCOTIC (MORPHINE NAR1 TMORPHPM)
          (DEMEROL NAR1 TDEM)
          (FENTANYL NAR1 TFENT))
(NAR1 (POP T T))


(SED2 (BARBITURATE SED3 TBARB)
      (VALIUM SED3 TVAL)
      (DROPERIDOL SED3 TDROP)
      (VISTARIL SED3 TVIST)
      (PHENERGAN SED3 TPHEN)
      (NOSEDATIVE1 SED3 TNOSED1))
(SED3 (POP T T))
```

```
(ANTICHOL (ATROPINE ANT1 TATR)
          (GLYCOPYRROLATE ANT1 TROB))
(ANT1 (POP T T))


(BARBITURATE (PENTOBARBITAL BAR1 TPENTO)
             (SECONAL BAR1 TSEC))
(BAR1 (POP T T))


(CONDUCTION (EPIDURAL CND1 TEPID)
            (SPINAL CND1 TSPINAL))
(CND1 (POP T T))


(REGIONAL (CONDUCTION REG1 TCONDUCT)
          (NB REG1 TNB))
(REG1 (POP T T))


(EPIDURAL (NESACAINE EP1 TNES)
          (MARCAINE EP1 TMARC)
          (LIDOCAINE EP1 TLIDO))
(EP1 (POP T T))


(SPINAL (TETRACAINE SP1 TTET)
        (LIDOCAINE SP1 TSPLIDO))
(SP1 (POP T T))


(NB (NESACAINE NB1 TNES)
    (MARCAINE NB1 TMARC)
    (LIDOCAINE NB1 TLIDO))
(NB1 (POP T T))
```

Appendix III Sample problem management frames

Appendix III shows how ATTENDING stores its knowledge of the anesthetic implications of a patient's underlying medical problems. Associated with each problem (asthma, chronic renal failure, and hypovolemia) is a list of management principles, followed by a list of risks.

The risks are represented as association lists (name-value pairs). Each risk indicates:

(a) the arc which it augments, which it indicates by naming the associated action routine,

(b) the risk magnitude (RISKVAL) which can be LOWR, MODR, HIGHR, etc. for a risk, or LOWB, MODB, etc for a benefit,

(c) one or more prose fragments describing the risk,

(d) additional information which the system uses for various purposes in processing the risk.

```
(DEFFRAME 'ASTHMA '(
PRINCIPLES (
    (PREFER DEEP_ANESTHESIA DANGER BRONCHOSPASM)
    (PREFER BRONCHODILATORS DANGER BRONCHOSPASM)
    (AVOID BRONCHOSPASTICS DANGER BRONCHOSPASM)
    )
RISKS (
    (ARC TRAPIDSEQ RISKVAL LOWR DESC (BRONCHOSPASM) WHENSEVERE T)
    (ARC TINHAL RISKVAL LOWB DESC (PREVENTING BRONCHOSPASM BY KEEPING THE
            ANESTHETIC LEVEL DEEP) WHENSEVERE T)
    (ARC THALO RISKVAL LOWB DESC (HELPING PREVENT BRONCHOSPASM SINCE
            HALOTHANE IS A BRONCHODILATOR) WHENSEVERE T)
    (ARC TKETAMINE RISKVAL MODB DESC (SUPPRESSING BRONCHOSPASM SINCE
            KETAMINE IS A BRONCHODILATOR) WHENSEVERE T)
```

```
(ARC TDTC RISKVAL LOWR DESC (BRONCHOSPASM) MECH HISTAMINE MECHDESC
        (TRIGGERED HISTAMINE RELEASE) WHENSEVERE T)
(ARC TMORPH RISKVAL LOWR DESC (BRONCHOSPASM) MECH HISTAMINE MECHDESC
        (DUE TO HISTAMINE RELEASE) WHENSEVERE T)
(ARC TMORPHPM RISKVAL LOWR DESC (BRONCHOSPASM) MECH HISTAMINE MECHDESC
        (DUE TO HISTAMINE RELEASE) WHENSEVERE T)
(ARC TETH RISKVAL LOWR DESC (INITIAL BRONCHOSPASM DUE TO AIRWAY
        IRRITABILITY) WHENSEVERE T)
(ARC TTPL RISKVAL LOWR DESC (BRONCHOSPASM) WHENSEVERE T)
(ARC TAWAKE RISKVAL MODR DESC (BRONCHOSPASM) WHENSEVERE T)
(ARC TBALANCED RISKVAL LOWR DESC (POSSIBLE BRONCHOSPASM DUE TO LIGHT
        ANESTHESIA))
(ARC TNOSED NOTCONTEXT (ACUTE_TRAUMA) RISKVAL MODR WHENSEVERE T DESC
        (PROBLEMS WITH THE PATIENT APOST_S ASTHMA))
)))


(DEFFRAME 'CRF '(
PRINCIPLES (
    (AVOID RENAL_TOXINS DANGER RENAL_DAMAGE)
    (AVOID RENAL_EXCRETED_DRUGS DANGER COMPROMISED_EXCRETION)
    )
RISKS (
    (ARC TETH RISKVAL LOWR DESC (RENAL TOXICITY DUE TO METABOLIC RELEASE OF
            FLUORIDE) QUESTRISK T)
    (ARC TGALL RISKVAL MODR DESC (PROLONGED POSTOPERATIVE PARALYSIS DUE TO
            COMPROMISED RENAL EXCRETION))
    (ARC THIGHPAV RISKVAL LOWR DESC (PROLONGED POSTOPERATIVE PARALYSIS DUE
            TO COMPROMISED RENAL EXCRETION))
    (ARC TDTC RISKVAL NONE WELLCHOS T DESC (IT IS RELIABLY METABOLIZED BY
            THE LIVER))
    (ARC THALO RISKVAL NONE WELLCHOS T DESC (IT HAS MINIMAL NEPHROTOXICITY))
    )))
```

```
(DEFFRAME 'HYPOVOLEMIA '(
PRINCIPLES (
    (AVOID HYPOTENSIVE_TECHNIQUES DANGER HYPOTENSION)
    (PREFER HYPERTENSIVE_TECHNIQUES DANGER HYPOTENSION)
    )
RISKS (
    (ARC TINHAL RISKVAL MODR DESC (HYPOTENSION) PROB HYPOVOLEMIA PROBDESC
        (IN THE PRESENCE OF HYPOVOLEMIA) TYPE HYPOTENSION)
    (ARC TINHALIN RISKVAL MODR DESC (HYPOTENSION) PROB HYPOVOLEMIA PROBDESC
        (IN THE PRESENCE OF HYPOVOLEMIA) TYPE HYPOTENSION)
    (ARC TTPL RISKVAL LOWR DESC (HYPOTENSION) PROB HYPOVOLEMIA PROBDESC (IN
        THE PRESENCE OF HYPOVOLEMIA) POSSRISK T TYPE HYPOTENSION)
    (ARC TDROP RISKVAL MODR DESC (HYPOTENSION) PROB HYPOVOLEMIA PROBDESC (IN
        THE  PRESENCE  OF  HYPOVOLEMIA)  MECH  ALPHABLOCK  MECHDESC  (DUE  TO
        ALPHA BLOCKADE) TYPE HYPOTENSION)
    (ARC TMORPH RISKVAL LOWR DESC (HYPOTENSION) PROB HYPOVOLEMIA PROBDESC
        (IN THE PRESENCE OF HYPOVOLEMIA) MECH HISTAMINE MECHDESC (SINCE
        MORPHINE CAN TRIGGER HISTAMINE RELEASE) TYPE HYPOTENSION)
    (ARC TDTC RISKVAL LOWR DESC (HYPOTENSION) PROB HYPOVOLEMIA PROBDESC (IN
        THE PRESENCE OF HYPOVOLEMIA) MECH HISTAMINE MECHDESC (SINCE CURARE
        CAN INDUCE HISTAMINE RELEASE) TYPE HYPOTENSION)
    (ARC KETAMINE RISKVAL MODB DESC (HELPING AVOID HYPOTENSION SINCE
        KETAMINE IS SUPPORTIVE OF BLOOD PRESSURE))
    (ARC TBALANCED RISKVAL LOWB DESC (MAINTAINING BLOOD PRESSURE) PROB
        HYPOVOLEMIA PROBDESC (IN THE PRESENCE OF HYPOVOLEMIA))
    (ARC TCONDUCT RISKVAL HIGHR DESC (SEVERE HYPOTENSION DUE TO
        SYMPATHECTOMY)  PROB  HYPOVOLEMIA  PROBDESC  (IN  A  HYPOVOLEMIC
        PATIENT) TYPE HYPOTENSION)
    )))
```

References

Aikins, J.S., Kunz, J.C., Shortliffe, E.H., Fallat, R.J.   PUFF: An
    experimental system for interpretation of pulmonary function data.
    Computers and Biomedical Res. 16(1983) 199-208.

Appelt, D.   Planning natural language utterances to satisfy multiple
    goals. (Ph.D. thesis, Stanford: Stanford University, 1982).

Blum, R.L.   Discovery, confirmation, and incorporation of causal
    relationships from a large time-oriented clinical data base: The RX
    project.   Computers and Biomedical Res. 15(1982) 164-187.

Buchanan, B.G., and Feigenbaum, E.A.   DENDRAL and Meta-DENDRAL: Their
    applications dimension. Artificial Intell. 11(1978) 5-24.

Buchanan, B.G., and Shortliffe, E.H.   Rule-based expert systems: The MYCIN
    experiments of the Heuristic Programming Project. (Reading:
    Addison-Wesley, 1983).

Campbell, A.N., Hollister, V.F., Duda, R.O., Hart, P.E.   Recognition of a
    hidden mineral deposit by an artificial intelligence program. Science
    217(1982) 927-929.

Chandrasekaran, B., Mittal, S., Smith J.S.   Reasoning with uncertain
    knowledge: The MDX approach. In: Proceedings of the American Medical
    Informatics Association Congress-82, San Francisco (1982) 335-339.

Clancey, W.J., and Letsinger, R.   NEOMYCIN: Reconfiguring a rule-based
    expert system for application to teaching. Proceedings of the Seventh
    International Joint Conference on Artificial Intelligence, Vancouver
    (1981) 829-836.

Clancey, W.J. and Shortliffe, E.H. (eds)   Readings in medical artificial
        intelligence: the first decade. (Reading: Addison-Wesley, 1984).

Davis, R.   Meta-rules: Reasoning about control. Artificial Intell.
        15(1980) 179-222.

Davis, R. and Lenat, D.B.   Knowledge based systems in artificial
        intelligence. (New York: McGraw Hill, 1982).

Drastal, G., and Kulikowski, C.   Knowledge-based acquisition of rules for
        medical diagnosis. J.Med.Systems 6(1982) 433-445.

Duda, R.O. and Shortliffe, E.H.   Expert systems research. Science
        220(1983) 261-268.

Fagan, L.M., Kunz, J.C., Feigenbaum, E.A., Osborn, J.J.   Representation of
        dynamic clinical knowledge: Measurement interpretation in the
        intensive care unit. In: Proceedings of the Sixth International Joint
        Conference on Artificial Intelligence, Tokyo (1979) 260-262.

Gorry, G.A., Silverman, H., Pauker, S.G.   Capturing clinical expertise: A
        computer program that considers clinical responses to digitalis.
        Am.J.Med. 64(1978) 452-460.

Harrison, M.J., and Johnson, F.   Codifications of anesthetic information
        for computer processing. J.Biomed.Engr. 3(1981) 196-199.

Hayes-Roth, F., Waterman, D.A., Lenat, D.B.   Building expert systems.
        (Reading: Addison-Wesley, 1983).

Kastner, J., Weiss, S., Kulikowski, C.   Treatment selection and explanation
        in expert medical consultation: application to a model of ocular
        herpes simplex. In: Proceedings of MEDCOMP-82, Philadelphia (1982)
        420-427.

Kingsland, L.C., Gaston, L.W., Vanker, A.D., Lindberg, D.A.B.   A
    knowledge-based consultant system for problems in human hemostasis.
    In: Proceedings of the American Medical Informatics Association
    Congress-82, San Francisco (1982) 325-329.

Kingsland, L.C., and Lindberg, D.A.B.   Research methods in AI model
    building: The history of a project. In: Proceedings of AAMSI
    Congress-83, San Francisco (1983) 76-80.

Kulikowski, C.A.   Artificial intelligence methods and systems for medical
    consultation. IEEE Trans.PAMI PAMI-2(1980) 464-476.

Kulikowski, C.A., and Weiss, S.   Computer-based models for glaucoma.
    (CBM-TM-MS1, Rutgers University, 1971).

Langlotz, C.P. and Shortliffe, E.H.   Adapting a consultation system to
    critique user plans. International Journal of Man-Machine Studies
    (1983) in press.

Lindberg, D.A.B., Sharp, G.C., Kingsland, L.C., Weiss, S.M., Hayes, S.P.,
    Ueno, H., Hazelwood, S.E.   Computer based rheumatology consultant.
    In: Proceedings of MEDINFO-80, Philadelphia (1980) 1311-1315.

Lindsay, R.K., Buchanan, B.G., Feigenbaum, E.A., Lederberg, J.
    Applications of artificial intelligence for organic chemistry: The
    DENDRAL project. (New York: McGraw-Hill, 1980).

London, R., and Clancey, W.J.   Plan recognition strategies in student
    modelling: prediction and description. In: Proceedings of the American
    Association for Artificial Intelligence, Pittsburgh (1982) 335-338.

Materson, B.J., Oster, J.R., Michael, U.F., Bolton, S.M., Burton, Z.C.,
    Stambaugh, J.E., Morledge, J.   Dose response to chlorthalidone in
    patients with mild hypertension. Efficacy of a lower dose.
    Clin.Pharmacol.Ther. 24(1978) 192-198.

McDermott, J.   R1: A rule-based configurer of computer systems.
    Artificial Intell. 19(1982) 39-88.

McDonald, D.D.   Natural language production as a process of
    decision-making under constraint. (Ph.D. thesis, Cambridge: MIT, 1980).

McKeown, K.R.   Generating natural language text in response to questions
    about the data base structure. (Ph.D. thesis, Philadelphia: Moore
    School of Electrical Engineering, University of Pennsylvania, 1982).

Miller, P.L.   ATTENDING: a system which critiques an anesthetic management
    plan. In: Proceedings of the American Medical Informatics Association
    Congress-82, San Francisco (1982a) 36-40.

Miller, P.L.   PROSENET: Facilitating machine generation of prose analysis
    of medical management. In: Proceedings of MEDCOMP 82, Philadelphia
    (1982b) 460-464.

Miller, P.L.   A heuristic approach to risk analysis in computer-assisted
    medical management. In: Proceedings of the Sixth Symposium of Computer
    Applications in Medical Care, Washington, D.C. (1982c) 697-701.

Miller, P.L.   The ATTENDING system. In: Proceedings of MEDCOMP 82,
    Philadelphia (1982d) 409-412.

Miller, P.L.   ATTENDING: Critiquing a physician's management plan. IEEE
    Trans. PAMI PAMI-5(1983a) 449-461.

Miller, P.L.   Critiquing anesthetic management: the "ATTENDING" computer
    system. Anesthesiology 53(1983b) 362-369.

Miller, P.L.   Critiquing as a modality for computer advice in medical
    management and work-up. In: Proceedings of the Seventh Symposium on
    Computer Applications in Medical Care, Baltimore (1983c) 842-843.

Miller, P.L., Angers, D., Marks, P., Sudan, N., Tanner, G.   Teaching with
"ATTENDING": a practical way to "debug" an expert knowledge base. In:
Proceedings of the American Association for Medical Systems and
Informatics Congress-83, San Francisco (1983d) 87-91.

Miller, P.L.   Critiquing as a modality for explanation: Three systems.
In: Proceedings of the Amercian Association for Medical Systems and
Informatics Congress-84, San Francisco (1984a) in press.

Miller, P.L.   Expert consultation systems in medicine. In: Proceedings of
the Sixth Annual International Symposium on Computers in Critical Care
and Pulmonary Medicine, Heidelberg (1984b) in press.

Miller, P.L. and Black, H.R.   Medical plan-analysis by computer:
Critiquing the pharmacologic management of essential hypertension.
Computers and Biomedical Res. 17(1984) 38-54.

Miller, M.L., and Goldstein, I.   Structured planning and debugging. In:
Proceedings of the Fifth International Joint Conference on Artificial
Intelligence, Boston (1977) 773-779.

Miller, R.A., Pople, H.E., Meyers, J.D.   Internist-I, an experimental
computer-based diagnostic consultant for general internal medicine.
N.Eng.J.Med. 307(1982) 468-476.

Nilsson, N.J.   Principles of artificial intelligence.   (Palo Alto: Tioga
Press, 1980).

Patil, R.S., Szolovits, P., Schwartz, W.B.   Causal understanding of patient
illness in medical diagnosis. In: Proceedings of the Seventh
International Joint Conference on Artificial Intelligence, Vancouver
(1981), 893-899.

Pauker, S.G., Gorry, G.A., Kassirer, J.P., Schwartz, W.B.   Towards the
simulation of clinical cognition: taking a present illness by
computer. Am.J.Med. 60(1976) 981-996.

Politakis, P., and Weiss, S.M.   A system for empirical experimentation with expert knowledge. Technical Rept. CBM-TM-091, Computer Science Department, Rutgers University, New Brunswick, N.J. (1981).

Pople, H.E.   Heuristic methods for imposing structure on ill-structured problems: The structuring of medical diagnostics in artificial intelligence in medicine.   In: Szolovits, P. (ed) Artificial Intelligence in Medicine. (Boulder: Westview Press, 1982).

Reggia, J.A.   A production rule system for neurological localization. In: Proceedings of the Second Annual Symposium on Computer Applications in Medical Care, Washington, D.C. (1978) 254-260.

Rich, C., Shrobe, H.E., Waters, R.C.   An overview of the programmer's apprentice. In: Proceedings of the Sixth International Joint Conference on Artificial Intelligence, Tokyo (1979) 827-828.

Rich, E.   Artificial Intelligence. (New York: McGraw-Hill, 1983).

Sacerdoti, E.D.   A structure for plans and behavior. (New York: Elsevier, 1977).

Scott, A.C., Clancey, W.J., Davis, R., Shortliffe, E.H.   Explanation capabilities of production-based consultation systems. In: Clancey, W.J. and Shortliffe, E.H. (eds)   Readings in medical artificial intelligence: the first decade. (Reading: Addison-Wesley, 1983).

Shortliffe, E.H.   Computer-based medical consultations: MYCIN. (New York: American Elsevier, 1976).

Shortliffe, E.H., Buchanan, B.G., Feigenbaum, E.A.   Knowledge engineering for medical decision making A review of computer-based clinical decision aids. Proc.IEEE 67(1979) 1207-1224.

Shortliffe, E.H., Scott, A.C., Bischoff, M.B , Campbell, A.B., Van Melle, W., Jacobs, C.D. An expert system for oncology protocol management. In: Proceedings of the Seventh International Joint Conference on Artificial Intelligence, Vancouver (1981) 876-881.

Stefik, M. Planning with constraints (MOLGEN: part 1). Planning and meta-planning (MOLGEN: part 2). Artificial Intell. 16(1981) 111-170.

Stefik, M., Aikins, J., Balzer, R., Benoit, J., Birnbaum, L., Hayes-Roth, F., Sacerdoti, E.D. The organization of expert systems. Artificial Intell. 18(1982) 135-173.

Sussman, G.J. A computer model of skill acquisition. (New York: Elsevier, 1975).

Suwa, M., Scott, A.C., Shortliffe, E.H. An approach to verifying completeness and consistency in a rule-based expert system. AI Magazine 3(1982) 16-21.

Swartout, W.R. Explaining and justifying expert consultation programs. In: Proceedings of the Seventh International Joint Conference on Artificial Intelligence, Vancouver (1981) 815-822.

Swartout, W.R. GIST English generator. In: Proceedings of the National Conference on Artificial Intelligence, Pittsburgh (1982) 404-409.

Szolovits, P. (ed) Artificial intelligence in medicine. (Boulder: Westview Press, 1982).

Szolovits, P., and Pauker, S.G. Categorical and probabilistic reasoning in medical diagnosis. Artificial Intell. 11(1978) 115-144.

Teach, R.L. and Shortliffe, E.H. An analysis of physician attitudes regarding computer-based clinical consultation systems. Computers and Biomedical Res. 14(1981) 542-558.

van Melle, W.   A domain-independent production-rule system for consultation programs. In: Proceedings of the Sixth International Joint Conference on Artificial Intelligence, Tokyo (1979) 923-925.

Weinstein, M.C., Fineberg H.V., Elstein, A.S., Frazier, H.S., Neuhauser, D., Neutra, R.R., McNeil, B.J.   Clinical decision analysis. (Philadelphia: Saunders, 1980).

Weiss, S., and Kulikowski, C.   EXPERT: A system for developing consultation models. In: Proceedings of the Sixth International Joint Conference on Artificial Intelligence, Tokyo (1979) 942-950.

Weiss, S., Kulikowski, C., Amarel, S., Safir, A.   A model-based method for computer-aided medical decision-making. Artificial Intell. 11(1978) 145-172.

Weiss, S., Kulikowski, C., Galen, R.   Developing microprocessor based expert models for instrument interpretation. In: Proceedings of the Seventh International Joint Conference on Artificial Intelligence, Vancouver (1981) 853-855.

Winston, P.H.   Artificial intelligence.   (Reading: Addison-Wesley, 1977).

Winston, P.H., and Horn, B.K.P.   LISP. (Reading: Addison-Wesley, 1981).

Woods, W.A.   Transition network grammars for natural language analysis. CACM 13(1970) 591-606.

Acknowledgement

This research was supported in part by NIH Grant 03978 from the National Library of Medicine. It was performed using the SUMEX-AIM computer facility which is supported by the NIH Division of Research Resources. The material has been previously described in several articles and conference proceedings papers. Portions of this book have been adapted from (Miller 1982abcd, 1983acd, 1984ab) with copyright permission from the publishers.

The author would like to thank the numerous members of the SUMEX-AIM community who have offered comments and encouragement during the course of this research, including Drs. Casimir Kulikowski, Edward Shortliffe, Donald Lindberg, and Lawrence Kingsland III; the members of Yale's Department of Anesthesiology who have at times contributed to the project, including Philip Marks and Drs. Nicholas Greene, Denise Angers, Nalin Sudan, and Guy Tanner; and also Gail Norup and Linda Shiffrin who assisted in preparing the manuscript.

Index

relationship to preexisting user competence, 5

Decision tree, 40
DENDRAL, 13
Diagnosis, 13-15, 48, 72
    critiquing diagnosis, 83
    difficulties with computer assisted diagnosis, 21-22
Digitalis Advisor, 15

EMYCIN, 13
EXPERT, 15
Expert systems
    evaluation, 72-73, 77
    in medicine, 12
    introduction, 12
    validation, 72-73, 77
Explanation, 17, 18-19
    critiquing as explanation, 19, 74

GUIDON, 13, 71

Heuristic computation, 9
HT-ATTENDING, 79-80

INTERNIST, see CADUCEUS

Knowledge acquisition, 13, 20-21

LISP, 12, 94

Medical management
    advantages as a domain for computer assistance, 22-24
    critiquing medical management, 79-81
Medical workup, 82
MYCIN, 13, 17, 71

Natural language generation, 56
NEOMYCIN, 13, 71

ONCOCIN, 16, 81

Pharmacy information systems, 23
PIP, 15
Planning, 40
Pragmatic features, 51-53
Problem management frames, 33, 98-100
Production rules, 13, 17-18
PROSENET, 55-63
PUFF, 13, 16

Risk analysis, 43, 75
    heuristic risk analysis, 46-54, 76
    implementation in ATTENDING, 98-100
    relationship to critiquing, 65-67
    statistical risk analysis, 45

SPE, 15, 16
Subjectivity, sources in medicine, 3
Symbolic computation, 9

Teaching applications, see Computer-aided teaching
TEIRESIAS, 13

VM, 16
VQ-ATTENDING, 81